KVETCH: ONE BITCH OF A LIFE

"…Her memoir is remarkable for its unflinching honesty, along with a refusal to descend into sentimentality. Nevertheless, the work is both emotional and poignant— an unpredictable roller coaster ride along the rails of the human condition. Her story will grip you."—Stuart Isacoff, author of *Temperament* and *A Natural History of the Piano*.

Also By Greta Beigel

Mewsings: My Life as a Jewish Cat

A Jew from Riga

⌣‿⌐

Audio

Scholarship recital, piano

Mewsings: My Life as a Jewish Cat, Greta Beigel narrator, Michael Hoppe piano.

KVETCH:
ONE BITCH OF A LIFE

A Memoir of Music & Survival

GRETA BEIGEL

Copyright

ISBN-10: 0615940722
ISBN-13: 9780615940724
Library of Congress Control Number: 2014900583
Mons Road Press, Ashland, OR

<u>Cover Photo</u>: Pianist Greta Beigel in concert in Johannesburg, age 23.

CONTENTS

No. 37 Mons Road

We live in a mystery house at No. 37 Mons Road, in the suburb of Yeoville, Johannesburg, South Africa, the world. My mother wishes we were in Observatory with its nice houses and larger lawns over the hill, but technically we reside in poor old Yeoville and this makes her crazy.

I've just turned seven and guess what? I've started weekly piano lessons with Mrs. Segal. She lives in a double-story white house and styles her brown hair in a big fat bun. Musicians concur she does nicely as a first teacher for a little girl, but after two sessions Mrs. Segal flat out declares me a piano prodigy.

You could say my keyboard gifts presented themselves as an afterthought, really. My mother, desperate for acceptance amongst the Jews of Joh'burg—they judge her fat, frumpy, even dumb—remains determined to find a talent in me.

After all, talent can make a life special even gain entrée into rich society. First we try tap dancing.

"She's just like an elephant," Mommy relays to Fanny, her chain-smoking sister and my aunt with the flaxen hair. But I so enjoy the clack-clack of my feet; why must I take ballet instead? Within months of touching the piano, however, yours truly emerges a star, soon snaring top prizes at local eisteddfods, then national contests. The press takes note:

> *"This girl is a born musician. She is not just a good pianist; she has the makings of a very great pianist. Her talent should be carefully nursed,"* posits one writer for the evening Star.

My mother assumes control of my studies, in particular the choice of repertory. She exhibits little patience with the Preludes and Fugues of J.S. Bach, the very staple of pianism. Or the sonatas—"what; there are three movements to learn?"—of Mozart, Beethoven even Haydn. To the chagrin of my teachers—many vie to have me on their rosters—my mom insists on the glitzy showpieces of Chopin or Liszt, where a *wünderkind* can shine and win medals and trophies and land articles with photos in newspapers and the phone can ring for days on end and we all feel so important.

Following my every success, I swear Mommy stands taller. In that special falsetto voice, she brags about my wins at the nearby Teddy Bear Fisheries (and groceries) while selecting fresh sole to fry for Friday night's Sabbath dinner. And she fusses a little longer over that loaf of rye—"no, let's choose the brown bread today"—at the café on the corner.

Weekdays she awakens me around 6:30 to practice scales and assorted finger exercises before my ride pulls up to drive me to Barnato Park Primary School. When the bus drops me back home, I must put in another five-to-six hours of playing pieces. Then it's supper and homework. My day usually ends around 11 p.m. How old am I? Eight.

Mommy shows scant interest in my schoolwork. She pays great heed, however, to my brother's grades, demanding he *swot* for exams. Mostly, she drums into his psyche his main role in life: to support her financially, forever, and it better all commence sooner than later.

It's clear I'm good for one thing only: The Piano. Picture one winter's eve when my father—his name is Richard—sits smoking in the maroon-carpeted lounge. Pointing me to the brown upright in the corner, my mother declares: "Get stuck in, get stuck in and practice." Bored, an almost bitchy look on his face, my Dad keeps glancing at the mantelpiece where a small wooden replica of a ship with mast remains berthed. To my mother's bemusement, he takes the ship with him whenever he leaves; when the vessel rests in port, means Daddy's home.

According to my mother, in their first years together my father "cherished" her, making sure her hands were warm, her neck covered against cold. She can't fathom the change.

Now, whenever he packs his bags I'm required to vacate my bedroom with its white furniture in the front of the house and go sleep in the bed next to hers at back. Why should I? How will I find my things, especially my beloved Enid Blyton mystery books, you know the British ones about the adventures of the Famous Five and the Secret Seven? Oh, where would I be without these books? How would I survive?

Nightly, she storms my head with stories: How he likes to be on top of her and nearly "rape" her. (I may be little, but I'm smart and I can read and I know that word connotes something bad.) I hear how he punched her ears while she sat on the toilet in the half-bathroom, knocking her to the red-polished stone floor. And that late at night, when she lays down exhausted after putting us kids to bed, he yawns loudly and slaps his left arm across her face when she protests, "Richard, can't you see I'm trying to sleep?" (Years later, I made a point of studying my Father's famous yawns: To be fair, they could traverse an octave and go from *sotto voce* to a roar that would do the MGM lion proud.)

My brother inhabits a strange room at the back, near the rear porch. There's a brown bed and a brown wardrobe with ties hanging from a rack. I think he shares this space with Daddy, but can't be sure. He's sooooo scrawny. And there he is, the elder sibling, in every photo hugging me tight.

"He likes to protect Gitella," my mother says of the way my brother's arm surrounds my little frame. Apparently,

I started out as a fat baby rarely making noise or trouble. As I grew older, I grew to hate food. Did anyone ever find the steaks or omelets I threw out the bedroom window or buried beneath the double wardrobe in my parents' room? I wonder about that, still.

In our three-bedroom house, painted white with a red tile roof, there appears a mythical north/south divide. Rooms facing north provide sunny comfort in cold winters; the southern block, leads to all sorts of ill health. Johannesburg homes rarely feature central heating; stand-alone grilles that easily cause fires yield the only warmth. Most of us catch a cold or the flu every six-eight weeks; as a society we treat most ailments with antibiotics. "That's why we all look so washed out," my mother reasons. "It's these drugs, they cause a depression."

My bedroom may face south, the wrong side, but it overlooks a lovely lemon tree out front, and a little to the left, a rose garden that my mother with her green thumbs makes bloom bright in pinks and yellows and reds. I like standing next to her when she prunes the roses. She says little. I also enjoy playing at the back lawn where at one end an apricot tree with the thickest trunk sprawls outrageously and in obvious defiance of a curvaceous pear number beckoning from across the half-acre expanse. In between, peach and fig and assorted plum trees boast their bounties. We also lay claim to a parsley patch and a quince bush and most fun of all, a shaded grapevine, where I play cards and even dollhouse with my friend Phyllis, the one with the sweet smile and curly light-brown hair.

My favorite game of all time? "Conductor, conductor." Hip settled on a perch in the pear tree, I metamorphose into a bus or tram inspector/conductor, replete with pretend money belt for taking tickets or giving change. To signal the driver, I yank on the laundry line stretching from the red plum tree to above my head. One "ting" indicates a stop; "Ting, ting," gives the ok to proceed.

What bliss, that is until I start fainting/falling in the hot sun. Plop. Strangely, Mommy's also experiencing similar spells. You know she's weak and fragile. If she faints, I must revive her soonest with a nip from the brown brandy bottle located in the lounge. "Never let me fall asleep," she instructs.

But should our world collapse, we know we can count on our nanny to pick us up. Sophie Mputi, that pudgy-cheeked Sotho girl with the creamy skin and gleaming white teeth came to work for my mother when I was seven. Inexplicably, I named her "Kweekie." Under the formalities of apartheid, she respectfully refers to my mother as "Missee." Any male authority figure ranks either "Master" or "Baas." For whatever reason, my moniker "Bee" endures.

Kweekie lives in the servants' quarters attached to the back of the house. She has a bathroom with running cold water. I don't know if there's anything hot. She works strange hours, on duty at 7 a.m. in a starched white apron and matching cap. Native women dare not show any dreadlocks; African heads in this city stay covered in shame. Kweekie makes us breakfast, usually eggs scrambled with tomatoes and served with hot dry toast—I loathe butter—and cups of brewed tea, then helps get us ready for school and my mother for work.

With us all out the house, Kweekie must dust. She gets into trouble for missing spots, especially after my mother runs her fingers along a lamp table in search of evidence of a job poorly done. Kweekie does all the washing by hand in the sink. I can see her scrubbing sheets on a washboard before hauling them out to dry on the line out back.

She gets off Saturday afternoons and some Sundays and entertains many gentleman callers, eventually marrying handsome Willie, the painter. However, under South Africa's strict apartheid laws, Willie dare not stay the night. He carries the dreaded identity "pass book," lest he be picked up by police and thrown in jail.

As a child I fail to comprehend why we're so pampered when ill, yet if Kweekie has a cold, she's required to show up. She gives us our medicines and takes my working mother's frantic phone calls. Why can't she also rest in bed? Mostly, I admire Kweekie's ability to balance on her turbaned head tubs of washing or dishes and glasses and bottles and still walk around with a perfect comportment. She often joins her Bantu and Zulu buddies on street corners to gossip, even sing and dance and revel in native rhythms. We whites just look on. Nothing special here.

After school, I often find Kweekie with Mommy slaving over the white stove, canning provisions for the winter months ahead. They add piles of white sugar to boiling water, huffing and puffing while they stir the giant pots. Mommy groans over those glass and rubber lids that refuse to properly seal the fruit or jam in jars. She's in another world, hardly available for questions or fun.

I'll test her. Playing hopscotch outside the kitchen door, I deliberately start screaming. Think she'll notice? My mother races outside. What's the matter? "Oh, I pretended, Mommy, just to see if you would come." She shakes her brown curls, merely resumes canning. I continue my jumps around the chalk.

She appears frantic, however, the afternoon she pulls up in a friend's car to find my brother in the street crying, both arms limp at his side. "It's polio," she screams at Mrs. Fishman. No, my *bootie* fell from his bike and broke both arms. He walks around for months with plaster casts on both sides.

Talking of bicycles. I got a metallic green variety for my birthday. Nobody has taught me how to ride, and last week I felt the whoosh of a speeding car coming towards me on the other side as I cycled fast down Mons Road. I don't remember getting home. But today my brother's with me in the backyard, showing me how to properly ascend the black padded seat. Oh look, there's Mommy. Oh, oh, she's flushed all red and glaring from the lounge window overlooking the little green hedge.

"Go on, you bit of rubbish you," she snarls. Brother speeds off. What happened? Why did he have to go? She's probably just mouthing one of her dreaded sayings, that's all. My mother has an arsenal of ready-to-aim missiles, including but not limited to:

"Go onnnnnn you bit 'o rubbish you";
"Go on, you rotter";
"Go on; you're just like your father" (reserved for my brother);
"Go on you little bitch" (all mine), and
"Hmmmm, God, is watching,"... "Godddd (crescendo) *will get you"* (Also mine).

Every eight months or so, my mother talks briefly of the birth and death of a first son, Bernard, when she was married a mere two years. She recounts how following Bernard's death, she sat crying alone on a park bench when a stranger approached. He comforted her, assuring the boy would have had a terrible time with his deformity and it all had happened for the best.

Uncle Louis (pronounced Lewey), Mommy's brother, later informs that the baby was born with a genital defect and the hospital fought hard for his life. Louis says my mom "went crazy" after the death. I wish I knew more about Bernard. What did he die of? Where is he buried? Would my mother have been different had her first-born survived? Would I be here?

My mother places the failure of the marriage with a couple of Jewish grouches who live nearby. In particular, she blames Mrs. Ray Groll, a small woman with a growling voice and fake fur for luring my father away nightly to play cards. "He's off to gamble with the Grolls," my mother complains.

Was he busy at poker that night I was born? My mom likes to regale how, after learning of the pregnancy, she'd lie on their bed and pound her stomach with a hangar: "Die, die, die," she yelled at me. I didn't get the message because apparently she labored for 17 hours before I arrived. (Whenever I see a program about babies bonding cheek-to-cheek, skin-to-skin, I weep knowing I had none of that.) Richard, your father, she likes to reiterate, failed to show up at my birth.

Relatives designate Richard a loser. Uncle Louis apparently used his many connections to place my Dad in various businesses but according to my mother, rather than work he spent afternoons striking up dalliances with women of all races—and this in apartheid South Africa. A "traveling" salesman, my father mocks my mother should she express joy at receiving steaks or other sundries in the wake of a successful week on the road. "You like that don't you?" he says, with a smirk.

Methinks Mommy pulls off miracles with her monies. She dresses us in the finest finery and keeps us clean. She believes babies should look inviting. She works only part-time, insisting that children always find a parent waiting when they return from school. She was there when my brother caught that awful whooping cough. She followed him for walks around the garden, watching his little body wrack with uncontrollable spasms.

Lucky for me she's home today. Looking all pretty, even sunny in my yellow and lace butterfly dress and matching panties, I've been invited to join my brother and his friend Barry from across the street in a special game at the back garden. Summer's here and the usual thundershowers expected. The boys take turns lying on the lawn; I have to run, gauntlet-style, and slowly, over their prostrate torsos. I don't like it, and go inside to tell.

"I'll talk to him," my mother says, drying her hands on an apron. She returns to the kitchen. "Don't worry, he won't do it again." She resumes rinsing the milk bottles.

Mommy believes that good food helps all. There's always fresh fruit and vegetables, and on Friday nights we taste either roasted chicken or grilled or fried fish courtesy of Kweekie's cooking. Worried about food poisoning, my mother soaks lettuce for hours on end. Come each December, she makes a big fuss as my birthday approaches, baking cupcakes, making jellies, buying ice cream and inviting cousins Brenda-Lee, Lynnette and Hedy-Anne and my friends to my party on the 29th. It makes me so happy. Yet she never talks about her own birthday. I still don't know when she was born.

But dinners at No. 37 Mons Road prove a somber affair. Mommy Mary glares at her husband who in turn accuses her of putting turnips into everything, from soup to stew. Meals at the formal dining room table conclude with canned fruits hauled from the cool kitchen pantry: sour red plums or bright yellow sweet peaches with grainy red centers or sour apricots topped with delicious dollops of frothy white cream.

Family lore has my father becoming enraged after one such dessert, chasing my brother down the passage and kicking him until the boy yelps, my mother running after, screaming, "I'll kill you Richard, you bastard you; I'll kill you if you touch my child again."

He never does, but we all hear about the boy's kidneys getting their kick—for the next 20 years.

Bar Mitzvah Boy

By far the most anticipated happening in our household ranks my 13-year-old brother's bar mitzvah. On the cusp of this coming-of-age-ritual, he's required to study Torah every afternoon at Hebrew school, never mind rugby or cricket or hanging out with his buddies. Do I have to go to *cheder*? Again?

My mother remains determined to compete with the Johannesburg Jews who fete their sons with lavish productions featuring garden marquees, fancy foods— and the discreet exchange of envelopes of money.

The very concept of celebration, however, remains anathema to my father. "That bastard; that bastard Richard won't lift a finger," according to my mother.

Seems all those decades ago growing up in the lovely city of Riga (Latvia), my Dad's bar mitzvah rated barely a blimp.

By his recount, as he stood shivering in the snow on this all-important day, his stern, ultra-Orthodox patriarch retrieved just-baked bread from the oven and, in an apparent rare softening, shoved a piece at the grateful 13-year-old: "Nah; Eat." End of ceremony.

But my mother persists with her plans for her son, and soon prevails upon her brother Louis, the chemist and self-made landowner who agrees to subsidize the grand event.

One week prior to his anointed rite of passage my brother catches the worst flu. Frantic, Mommy sets the alarm clock and every few hours, day or night plies him with prescribed pills, also cups of hot soup and cough mixture and a good tonic concocted by Uncle Louis. The Big Day dawns, and a pasty-looking boy in a navy suit and matching yarmulke enters Yeoville synagogue. Before a hushed community, he ascends to the *bima* to read the required portion. As befitting any Orthodox congregation, my mother in her new blue linen suit, with me on her knees, as well as all the invited women, watch the proceedings silently from upstairs; men participate in services down below. Meanwhile, my brother's pronouncements grow ever feeble.

Suddenly there's a gasp. Punkt, in the middle of the rabbi's blessing, he keels over. My mother rushes downstairs, cursing my rotten father. Everyone hurries to gather around the fainted bar mitzvah boy. I'm alone upstairs; I'll have to find my way back home. Why didn't they wait for me? I know. I'll retrace my steps along the route I take every Saturday with my brother when we come to shul. I'll run past the loquat tree, this day not stopping to taste of the sour orange fruit. Run past the white house with gray trim of Mrs. Gertrude Harvey Cohen and past the corner café. At last, I turn right and there's Mons Road and back to our house at No. 37. None of the aunts, uncles, cousins or celebrants says welcome back. No one noticed I was missing. Eating and drinking merely continues in the tent at the garden at the back.

This day, I suppose, my brother becomes a man. Then Daddy leaves. And so do we.

Your Father Left You On A Park Bench

A few weeks after my 10th birthday we move out, only to decamp for the next decade in a dingy two-bedroom flat bearing the romantic misnomer, "Glen Isle."

It's a royal given that I'll share the front bedroom with Mommy; my brother's relegated to his own space at back. If you decide to come and visit, go via the garage to where the garbage cans are stashed, stand up and peer through lace curtains and you'll see into his room. It's devoid of all sunlight.

At least as a teen my brother has his privacy. My mother goes on and on how the poor boy has no father to take him to soccer or rugby matches. And you should hear her when her son loses his place on the school cricket team. "Oh, his suffering," she laments to the world. Can you imagine what

17

she'd do if I said out loud hey, I also want/need a father? She'd kill me there and then. You know she would.

Now grown up, whenever I visit England and observe children on playing fields, a sense of déjà vu aches through my veins, transporting me to days of yore at King Edward's preparatory school where my brother hung around with pals Ozzie, Allan, Dickie and Mayer, all in their gray shorts and green V-neck jerseys. Observing cricketers in white pants and pressed shirts stepping up to bat, I hark back to those all-important cricket seasons, when the Brits or Aussies, even New Zealanders came out to play, causing commerce to cease and radio-toting South Africans to obsess over the latest scores.

Us Colonials had much in common with our British rulers that is until South Africa declared itself a republic in 1961. We used to celebrate the Queen's birthday with a 21-gun salute, and schools closed when Prince Charles and the other royals were born. I too wanted to be born into privilege; I desperately wanted to be Princess Anne. But luckily African subjects remained privy to the same delectable treats—Rowntree's fruit pastilles, Crunchies, Flake's, Peppermint Crisps, Aero slabs, white Nestlé chocolates—as other sweet-toothed counterparts throughout the Empire.

My mother, concerned over the many hours I spend at the piano, long demands that for exercise I walk home from school. Clad in my uniform—a revolting black tunic, matching stockings and beret in winter; white cotton dress and Panama in summer—I wander the streets alone, past the shops and swimming complex on busy Raleigh Street, past countless houses and gardens and children kicking ball. Where do I fit in? Hello, is anybody out there? Decades may pass, yet the sameness and routines of suburbia still can trigger a panic in me.

I hunger for diverse/exciting architecture, landscaping and certainly aesthetics. I can revel in the mysteries of say a Gothic arts center in Christchurch, New Zealand, and my senses almost merge with the sea and sun and those jutting planes of the Sydney Opera House and waterfront.

But put me midst nice Jewish ladies on manicured lawns of an elite Vancouver suburb, or with soccer moms at a field in northern London, or at small housing tracts in Culver City, LA, and yes, even on a quiet cul-de-sac framed by colorful houses in Reykjavik, Iceland, and I roil in terror.

As I do when remembering life at our gloomy suburban flat in Joh'burg. Scant visitors knock on our ground-floor door. Except for Daddy. When the divorce becomes final, he comes by regularly to take me to bioscope (the cinema) or out for milkshakes. "Do you know how much I love you? Do you, my Gitella?"

Last weekend we went to see a cartoon. We had great fun, and later parked across the street from the entrance to our flat. Suddenly, I remembered my instructions: I was to cry, beg him to come back to us. Looking to the right, I could feel Her presence peering from behind bedroom blinds.

"Please come home Daddy, we miss you," I tried hard to cry. He laughed. A lot.

"What did he say? What did Richard have to say?" When I relay Richard's response, my mother does something she's never done: She slaps my face.

Did I tell you my Dad was very handsome in his youth? I glean this much upon discovering photos that for years lay pasted and unobserved in a scrapbook my mother kept all to herself. There he stands, dapper at about 5'10", with hair thick and slick, teeth shining and white (that was before he got falsies). In one photo, cigarette dangling, he's sporting a creamy white shirt and matching creased pants. On his wedding day, his hooded baby browns stare teasingly at the camera, while he holds my flapper-modded mom so dearly. In a later and telling picture, she's captured walking solo in a stylish white and brown suit with matching pumps; that paper's serrated edges reveal that someone's missing, been slashed no doubt from visual memory.

They spend their honeymoon in popular Lourenço Marques, then-capital of Mozambique. Bride and groom dance to my mother's favorite waltz, "Fascination." I often find Mommy at the keyboard playing and singing that song, her thoughts a million miles away as though transported to the beginning when all apparently was fine with their union.

I'm at that shiny black grand late one afternoon perfecting runs in Mozart's lovely Rondo in D—it's not as easy as it looks or sounds—when my heart literally jumps in my chest. There's Mommy, all flushed and absurd in her fat-hiding blue linen suit, vaulting over the balcony. In one mad swoop she descends on me:

"Your father has deserted you; he's left you."
Huh?
"Your father abandoned you on a park bench."

Sobbing, she screams something about having climbed 1,000 steps to reach the parliamentary offices at the Union Buildings in the capital city of Pretoria (she could have bloody-well taken a taxi to the front entrance) to see a minister in an attempt to stop my father from leaving the country. She was too late. Her ex-husband already had set sail for America. I knew nothing of her/his mission.

Seems an employee at the American Consulate in downtown Johannesburg had promised to keep my suspecting mother apprised the very instant my father applied for a visa. There arrived no such notification.

Only the previous Saturday afternoon I met Daddy at the corner café. He bought me a vanilla cone and we hugged and laughed on the bench outside. There was no mention of any departure pending. Three days hence, he boarded ship with a relative from Eastern Europe who promised matrimony. My Dad subsequently did what my mother feared most: Abandoned all financial and whatever other responsibilities are required in the raising of offspring.

"Your father left you; he left you on a park bench."
I didn't get it then, but my Dad's dastardly deeds ultimately would save my life.

Who's The Monster?

For all our days neither my brother nor me are allowed to utter the word, "Daddy." Forget father. His very memory's stamped verboten in our house, our psyches, our very souls. Unless, of course, she feels like trotting him out for a good rant and rave and to remind, "the swine" never sends child support.

In my 11th year I find a new love. I rush home from school to say hi to Peter, the beautiful little budgie my mother bought for me especially, and who awaits my daily return in his new blue-painted cage. Oh how I love this little yellow bird. All morning I dream of feeding him. I have a few concerts coming up, and a lot of practicing to do, but first I want to kiss my little Peter.

I enter my brother's bedroom and look inside the cage. To my astonishment—then horror—the fragile yellow face is not there to greet me, but in its place, a great big old fat green owl. Or so it seems.

"Where's Peter?"

"That's Peter," my mother insists.

"No it isn't; where's Peter? Where's my birdie?" I'm crying hard now.

My mother confesses all. Apparently my brother had taken the cage out on the patio for cleaning; Peter somehow escaped the hatch and flew away. My brother, she assures, had done his best to catch him in the treetops. They'd rushed to the pet store and planted the substitute before I returned.

I can't breathe; I must lie down. Twenty minutes later my mother declares grief time over: "Now that's enough crying; go and practice," she says. Soon I hear her on the phone telling a friend about her crisis and laughing at what to do with a talented prodigy with an upcoming concert who's overwhelmed at the loss of a bird.

ODE TO CLAIR DE LUNE

I admit it. I fit the profile of a child prodigy. We kids accomplish amazing technical feats, without much thought. For a gifted prodigy to grow beyond innocence and into maturity as an artist, many factors must come into play: Having the right teacher(s), a nurturing home environment and strong interaction with like minds and beings. Lots of money also helps. Then of course there's luck....

I claim few of the above. Let's face it, if you're a good teacher in Europe or the States would you schlep down to the southern tip of Africa to foster your career? And if enlightened, risk your reputation being associated with a country that promotes racial prejudice? The few who do gravitate from abroad come mostly for the climate, but inevitably leave after a short tenure.

As a budding teen, I long to mix with great minds and for contact with musicians exposed to American culture.

But the top teachers where I live largely represent the home-grown variety, those who have studied overseas and returned conquering heroes. Mommy's determined to give me the best tuition available, happy to pay top monies.

Weekly, I journey downtown by bus for lessons with Brigitte Wild, a large Germanic import who claims to have studied with piano legend Claudio Arrau. Mrs. Wild, who soon moves on to teach in London, espouses the method of high finger articulation and demands her students spend hours practicing scales with curved fingers and those (later) much-maligned Hanon exercises. We discuss possible new pieces. She wants a Bach Partita.

"Well, I thought I could do 'Clair de Lune,'" I stutter, making my mother's demand that I learn the Claude Debussy favorite sound like my idea. Mrs. Wild starts screaming and my heart drops as always when someone quickly pierces the veil of my mother's pathetic vision. Mrs. Wild goes on to make her displeasure felt by beating rhythmic time on my fragile back far harder than usual.

Well, I do include "Clair de Lune" in recitals for many years to come, and ultimately deem the piece not too displeasing. I believe I add new gravitas to the concept of *schmaltz*.

To my mother, music theory, harmony, history and form remain extraneous nuisances rather than vital disciplines to be approached with respect, even joy. However, she arranges for me to study theory with one, Miss Hyams, a 75-year-old-plus biddy that I hope rots in whatsizname.

Terrified, I walk around the block three times before ringing the bell to Hyams' single flat in busy Berea. The wiry woman decorates her wispy white hair with an absurd, for such an ogre, little velvet ribbon, usually pink. We sit side-by-side at a round brown table in her living-cum-dining-cum-bedroom. Here, lace doilies cover the pink couch and rest under lamps or peek behind glass vases. She dips her quill pen into a little pale blue inkpot and scratches treble clefs on a sheet of manuscript.

If I name a wrong note, she pounds so hard the table shakes. She smashes the piano keys if I fail to correctly call a chord or an interval. My mom laughs at these antics, and enjoys sharing Miss Hyams horrorshlock with other mothers on the music circuit. I circle the blocks for many years, procrastinating and praying for a miracle. None transpire. I merely remain suspicious of solfège and forever incapable of integrating melody, harmony and counterpoint into my world.

In our household, making music remains über serious. Every media review constitutes life or death. Any hint of criticism gets analyzed, worse obsessed over. In the Rand Daily Mail on March 12, 1957, critic Dora Sowden notes of my participation in a student recital: *"Greta Beigel had sensitive touch and style in Mozart. When she learns to convey interest in the work as a whole and not merely in melodic sections, she should do well."* For years we debate the potency of these remarks.

But then Mommy cultivates no big picture. With little respect for artistic development, instant product matters most; to her competing, no winning, ranks supreme. Approach my mother with a new thought, an exciting concept and she'll raise her hand and swat your creative urge away with, "ah, please man; don't come here with your rubbish."

As much as she relishes applause, it becomes clear that Mommy needs me to excel only in her own backyard, her postage-stamp visage of the world, and I come to believe, solely to impress her siblings Louis, Abe, Fanny and naturally Bessie, the beautiful one.

Immediately after my any success she rushes home, picks up the phone and dials:
a) The media, then
b) Her envying brothers and sisters and their kids.

"Oh Louis, Louis, Greta won the medal; Greta won a silver trophy."
"Abe, Greta got the bursary."
Eyes twitching, she imbibes any compliments: "Oh, Bessie, yes, isn't it wonderful?" "Oh Fanny, Fankela, thank you *soooo* much."

It's a given that I'll shine scholastically, yet my mother scarcely notices my report cards or my struggles with silly knitting or sewing or home cooking, let alone the school's recommendation that I show gifts in French and should continue my studies.

I also reveal an early promise in tennis and revel in those after school classes with Mrs. Norgarb.

"You shhhtupid girl, don't just shhhtand dere like a cabbach," she chides when we miss a shot. But mostly I love the power of a good lobby. Then I make a critical error. I tell my mother that piano teacher Mrs. Wild deems tennis a strain for the wrists and generally not a good idea for pianists. That theory hardly has been supported. But my mom immediately kills the game.

In December, when the final exam results are announced at school, I dutifully place near the top of my class, tying for honors with friend Leila. She's also short, and lives mere blocks away from school in a pink house. After years of being my best pal Leila opts to hang out with the beautiful girls at school and dumps me. No fights, no animosity. She just fades away. And I miss her. However, her mom, with a sweet smile and golden wavy hair, always can be counted at home, teaching piano on a brown upright in the living room and offering cups of tea with talk.

Thinking no doubt of her own thwarted musicality, Leila's lovely mother likes to cite a phrase that will prove strangely prophetic: "Remember Greta," she says without provocation, "it's better to have been a has-been, than a never wasser."

WE'RE ALL SHOOK UP

In 1956 my insides change. Hell, the whole world changes. Elvis Presley has burst on the scene and nothing's the same. Not for me, my friends even my brother.

I first become aware of changes in the wind upon hearing Bill Hailey's "Rock Around the Clock." But nothing has prepared me for Presley's "Hound Dog." I'm shocked, even disgusted by the raw crudity of it all. And when he follows with "Don't be Cruel," I can't believe my ears. How does he get away with those indistinguishable inflections? And those slurred, imperfect phrases?

Many afternoons in Joh'ies, I relax on the white bench fronting our little flat and devour the latest Elvis glossies that reach our shores months after the rest of the world. I salivate over one shot of Elvis recording at Sun studios in Memphis. Oh God, I wish I was there; I'd kill to live in America.

In 1957 I too enter the recording booth, taping my first program for the South African Broadcasting Corporation. Settling on the black polished piano bench, back arched, breath drawn and hands poised, I await the green light flashing to red before beginning a Mozart Fantasia. A fortnight later, with my first paycheck from that radio recital, I visit the record shop downtown and buy Elvis's latest album, "Loving You." My mom acts as though the choice is the norm for a classical musician. My favorite track of all time, "Got a Lot o' Livin' to Do!" explodes with such exuberance that I feel propelled into my own life force.

During my rare time off on Saturday afternoons, I loll with friends at the public swimming pool debating the merits of Elvis's music. Like desperate, hungry animals we await any new release that immediately shoots to the top of the South African charts. I also resonate with some of the more poignant showstoppers: the lyrics to "Doncha' Think It's Time," or "The Girl of My Best Friend," provoke an inexplicable sense of yearning, while the raucous "Let's Have a Party," makes me want to go out and…..

My brother orders music magazines from England, and afternoons we pore over pages comparing thoughts and impressions of British rockers Cliff Richard, Tommy Steele and all those luscious '60s icons. Shirt open to the waist, my brother likes to front a makeshift mike, fantasizing as he recreates the sounds of the latest chart-toppers.

Does Mommy even register the revolution rockin' our generation? When I come home from a Tommy Steele concert and tell her we were hosed down by the cops and I could right now be in jail, she merely mutters, "Go and wash your hands for dinner." But then, conformity to her is everything; a rugged individualism, hell any kind of individuality ignites an immediate shame. What would have happened had she been Elvis's mom? Can you imagine if he showed up with his slicked hair and pink jackets and charcoal pants? She'd have killed his pelvic thrusts, then herself.

My mother fails to tolerate my brother's feeble attempt at fashion statement, in particular at age 14 when he begins sporting a cool, wayward sexy brown lock. She follows him around the house, or around the houses of relatives, mocking:
"There was a little boy,
Who had a little curl,
Right in the middle of his forehead..."
To make her point, she twists that little curl. How he doesn't belt her in the mouth, I will never know.

But mostly it's her son's jawline that my mother deems unacceptable. He obviously has inherited my father's bite, jutting forward (a la rocker Bruce Springsteen). After much inquiry, my mother decides on an innovative surgery that should push the protrusion back to a more pleasing position. It's all systems go, until a stranger appears at our door. He's from the university dental school, and pleads with my mother not to put her son's life in jeopardy with an untested procedure. She shakes her curls and my brother gets to keep his jaw.

APARTHEID...

I miss my older sibling at night. He often stays away at buddy Dickie or Meyer or Ozzie's house. I need his protection somehow. Is it Mommy I fear most? She bothers me less when he's around; otherwise she demands, enunciating slowly and in authoritarian tones that I must have supper with her. "You will sit with me at the table....." I clench my jaw; she masticates every single bite, in sadistic slow motion. Hours later when I finish my homework—I work at the dinner table—and go to the bedroom we share, she continues her cursing.

Under cover of darkness a secondary terror rages forth: the abuses of apartheid. Often my mom wakens me, beckoning me to the window. Fingers to lips, we watch members of the Afrikaner police force as they conduct raids and make arrests and throw African men into the backs of waiting vans, as though they're nothing more than sacks of *mealies* to be stacked up one against the other for transport.

For what? These men apparently are guilty of walking around without the requisite "pass books" documenting their existence. They can be stopped and picked off the streets at any time and in any place, and if failing to show reference books, detained. Whites for the most part merely look on, or cluck-cluck or perhaps even deem it all a good idea. I often hear shouting from upstairs as a husband or lover or friend of a servant employed by someone in the building is cornered and carted off by yet another zealous copper.

History note: In 1947, the Nationalist Party comes to power. This Afrikaner govt. soon begins its diatribes against Indians, "Coloreds" and Africans. The Dutch Reform Church sanctifies this apartheid, or apartness. Now the church makes damn sure that everything shuts down on Sundays and that cinemas and shops and places to eat remain closed. They make sure there's bugger-all for all of us to do. Except go to church, I suppose. Sex ranks next on the agenda, and the passage of the Immorality Act mandates sex between whites and non-whites illegal.

Mornings, Johannesburg streets are jammed with giant green Putco buses packed to capacity with non-white workers streaming into the city to work as domestics or gardeners. Evenings, the train station in Hillbrow remains chaotic with workers rushing along non-white platforms to catch trains alarmingly stacked to the rafters as they head back to Alexandra or Soweto townships with their shanties and smokestacks and no water or electricity and marauding *tsotsis*.

By contrast, whites-only platforms stand clean and orderly and calm. At virtually all public facilities, separate entrances exist for *blankes* and *nie-blankes*. Signs are posted in front of banks and at government buildings and outside post offices. Ironically, the nie-blankes are there for the most part to buy stamps for the blankes, and yet they have to resort to their separate entrances and stand in separate lines to make these purchases. Beaches are marked separate, and park benches painted blankes-only. Restaurants, cinemas, theaters and concert halls remain the sole purview of us Caucasians.

After I turn 14, my beloved Kweekie goes missing. She's just no longer there. Mommy's acting strange about her fate. She does allow that Kweekie has been admitted for throat problems to Baragwanath, the excellent hospital for non-whites. My mother makes several anxious phone calls daily to ascertain her condition. Following a stay of many months Kweekie returns to us, but now talks only in a whisper, a condition that lasts forever. "They made an operation, but they never told me what they did," Kweekie later recalled.

Another history note: In 1958, the Government demands that women too carry reference books. As police checks mount, so do protests. In 1960, anti-pass demonstrations erupt throughout the land. One such emergence in the small black township of Sharpeville sparks riots and a massacre by police leading to national and international condemnation. The Government declares a state of emergency, assuming sweeping powers against alleged troublemakers.

We ignore it all. Few of us teens acknowledge the cataclysmic events taking place, but newspaper coverage is extensive and at private teas and suppers many talk about getting out before the real revolution comes. Meanwhile, we friends mature into womanhood and family life continues.

So do police crackdowns. In 1963, the Ninety-Day Detention Law passes followed by the Sabotage Law. We begin to fear the dreaded knocking on the door of the security forces. They conduct searches without warrants, haul people off and hide them for months without access to lawyers. Stories in the Rand Daily Mail, the Star and the Sunday Times document middle-of-the-night raids. As I write this, I still feel the panic. The 1967 Terrorism Act enhances government powers to arrest and detain without trial.

Many activists work hard at change. I only read about (there's no television yet) saboteurs fleeing across the borders and if lucky, making it to Israel or England. Overall, few among South Africa's Jewry—at least I don't know of any—question the official word.

Oh sure, at Sunday family tea gatherings at Uncle Louis' sprawling pad some mumble that given our history of persecution we could be more sympathetic. Soon chatter putters out, and we smile and welcome John, looking all respectful in his white apron, as he wheels in the silver tea trolley replete with silver tea service and fragile floral cups and matching saucers, also cakes on lace doilies and hot scones with strawberry jam, and we forget about it all for a while.

...And The Livin' Made Easy

These are good times in the land my mother likes to call, "God's own country." The climate's wonderful and life's breezy what with some cousins and friends in rich white suburbia employing a "domestic servant" to cook, another to clean, one to do the garden and yet another to look after the kids—all for a pittance thanks to apartheid.

South Africa may well be scorned for its policies of segregation, but in global outlook local Jewry hardly proves provincial or insular. Patriarchs travel overseas extensively, going solo for business or accompanied by exotic wifey-poohs on exotic journeys. Legends abound about businessmen leaving the country with money or diamonds or minerals to deposit abroad, building up nest eggs in Swiss banks or in Luxembourg or in tax havens in the Jersey Isles ahead of the trouble we speculate eventually will erupt. After-dinner discussions center on how much money so and so has—and has managed to get out. There's even hushed talk about Government spies lurking in money centers such as Geneva or in hotel lobbies or at airport lounges in Europe and the States, bent on entrapping over-confident, unsuspecting South Africans.

At the tea table talk focuses on fabulous trips taken to nearby Lourenço Marques (later Maputo) in Mozambique, or the Cape's Garden Route, or Mauritius or Victoria Falls or Kruger National Park. And what about those luxury sailings to Beirut or Dar es Salaam? At such times, our family nucleus grows silent. We have nothing to contribute; a sense of mutual deprivation envelops us all.

My mom's younger sibling, Louis, owns a chemist shop around the corner from our flat. He makes his money building/buying/investing in shopping centers, and fast becomes a big *macha i*n the Jewish community. On the board of the King David Schools, he loves showing off photos taken with Israeli Prime Minister David Ben-Gurion who often visits S.A.

Tall, with a shiny baldpate ever since I recall, Uncle Louis nervously cricks his neck. But that hardly crimps his reputed attraction with the local ladies. However, he stays married to Auntie Gertie, a dancer of considerable talent in her youth, whom the other family matriarchs deem cold and unfeeling. To add to it all, she has a car. A woman driver, no less. Decades later I connect with Gertie and Louis on a visit to their flat in England. Gertie, who will live well into her 90s, embraces the arts. So does Louis. He fancies himself a leading tenor, of sorts.

At family gatherings, Louis' children then grandchildren and later great-grandchildren, stare adoringly as he readily answers the call for yet another over-the-top, throbbing delivery of the song, *"My Yiddishe Mama,"* as if anyone needs reminding of how much he adored his mother. Yes, that very matriarch who placed my mother and her sister Fanny—two out of six kids—in an orphanage for a few years. I often wonder what governed her selection process.

Local Jewish lore falsely finds Louis looking out for one of his own. "I can't imagine why Mary always was so worried about money all the time," the 80-something Louis postulates with me many years later in London, recalling my mother's ongoing and obvious insecurities. Louis also disclaims any recollection of the heady days when, as the young, good-looking and ambitious owner of Bedford Pharmacy he toyed with his sister.

Following my Dad's defection to America, my mother made what she repeatedly acknowledges as the biggest mistake of her life: She invested monies from the sale of the Mons Road home with Louis.

Monthly, she must go to the chemist shop to pick up her check. "I'm going to get my money from Louis," she mumbles, waving to me at the piano as she walks out the front door. It's always the same. She returns in about 20 minutes.

"Louis told me to come back later." She's flushed, looking sick. She goes to him three, four, five times over many days, begging for the money. He's busy or just rushing out, or doesn't have the cash and "please Merkela, come back later." The anguish on her face spells her humiliation. By the time Louis pays up, she's defeated.

One noontime while I'm practicing my mother returns home quietly and stops for a second, hand on the dining room door. "Dondela," she says, sounding the nickname she invented for me, her face contorted, "I never got the house. I suppose it was for the best."

Unbeknownst to me, she bid earlier that day for her dream house, a two-story beauty sitting on an acre in the sunny suburb she so loves, nearby Observatory. Damn, how she wants that white house. Every time we go by it, she wants it. I can only hazard how Louis negated her wishes. Mostly, I fantasize what might have been. I picture her puttering in her garden, raising roses with pride and abandon. I see her trimming the grass and sitting on the porch in the sun and maybe even smiling at her offspring with that vague look she owns when her thoughts stray too far away to articulate. Instead, her soul withers—along with her children's—in cramped rooms with little light and space and no greenery to call one's own.

Come Sunday nights, my mother often feels awful, especially if we've spent the afternoon at the plush home of our cousins in the luxurious suburb of Linksfield. The lush foliage, gorgeous bougainvillea, blue paradisiacal pool and swaying palms of their acreage must, I suppose, contrast horribly with our claustrophobic quarters.

My mom tries for cheery, opening cans of sardines, all glistening in oil, and places the silver slivers on toasted wheat bread with slices of tomato, then splashes her creations with malt vinegar. Oranges are sliced and lettuce leaves meticulously scrubbed again and again. Tea is brewed and finally ready.

Repast over, she's tearful and with what I now recognize as a habitual look of pure agony, turns to me: "Dondela, let's end it all. Let's put our heads in the oven." She doesn't hear me cackling inside, as I picture us two jostling for position what with her big bum sticking way out of the little gray antique stove.

A Passover Different From All Others

Each spring in our Orthodox household my mother together with Nanny Sophie Mputhi scrubs our house from top to bottom. And in keeping with the rules of a rapidly-approaching Passover, hauls out separate sets of dishes and utensils from the pantry, before removing all *chometz*, or leavened foods, from sight.

In preparation for the celebratory Seder meals, the two cook up their specialty: matzo balls, perfect rounds each with a sweet brown filling. Their recipe calls for frying onions in chicken fat until they turn a little brown, adding sugar, cinnamon, then squishing the lot into the middle of the matzo meal. My mother often boxes a half-dozen of these creations for transport by bus to the terminus in Pretoria where my anxious uncle Abe retrieves them for later presentation at his own Passover table.

Our little flat buzzes in anticipation of the festivities that mostly are shared with relatives and spread over two dinners, two luncheons and an afternoon tea. A first-night celebration at Uncle Louis and Auntie Gertie's house readily recalls in jolly and loud song the liberation of the Israelites from slavery in ancient Egypt.

Note the all-important Seder plate at the head of the table showcasing foods of great symbolism:

* *Karpa*s, a green vegetable, such as celery, parsley, cucumber, or radish or potato, to remind that Pesach coincides with the arrival of spring;
* *Maror*, either the head of a horseradish or some grated white horseradish, in remembrance of the bitterness of slavery, and
* *Charose*t, fruits, nuts and spices mixed with a little wine—my favorite; goes great on matzoh as an appetizer—to resemble the mortar used in making bricks to build Egyptian cities.

Unlike my cousins who attend a Jewish day school, I learn no Hebrew. As a consequence, I know only enough to join in the chorus of *"Day-yay-nu,"* a joyful Rondo expressing gratitude for the meal and our freedom as a people. But I have much fun later with *Chad gadya,* a folk tale about a dog, a cat, and a kid bought for two *zuzim* that goes on for many verses and smiles, and can easily be traversed in English or Hebrew.

Then the centerpiece: Four Questions examining the customs and foods of Passover that the youngest at the table must ask: "*Ma nishtana ha-laila ha-zeh mi-kol ha-laylot?* Why is this night different from all other nights?

What a contrast to the formality of a second-night Seder we attend at my beloved Aunt Fanny and Uncle Maish. (He's a radiologist with glasses who works at the hospital.) I'm placed next to my younger cousin Hedy-Anne, a fun-loving—the larger family calls her rebellious—teen with a space in her front teeth who sings and tap dances like no other.

Every word about the Exodus from Egypt is excruciatingly articulated from the *Haggadah* or prayer book. We depict the plagues being visited upon Pharaoh by dipping either a fork or a pinkie into a goblet, then placing a drop of wine into a saucer to represent: blood, frogs, lice, wild beasts, cattle plague, boils, hail, locusts, darkness and the 10th plague, which to this day sends shudders, the slaying of the firstborn. The ritual expresses our sympathy for the sufferings of the Egyptian people; nevertheless together with Hedy, I relish dipping, then flipping the red blots on to the plate, or if undetected, at each other.

At last the bit about the parting of the Red Sea, and then time for serving the gelatinous gefilte fish. I can't recall the soup, or even the main dish, but oh, what sweet escape to conclude all with Aunt Fanny's gushy white meringues that stick to our teeth.

But heaven help me should my mother receive no invitations for Seder. Oh sure, my nanny will slave all day and come up with plump matzo balls, as well as roast chicken and crispy roasted potatoes. But no prayers, no songs, no gratitude for the bounty of the table or for being with loved ones. "I swear something must have happened to her when she was young," my brother decides years later, "she's always crazy around Pesach."

At our homegrown Seder, the air resonates with deprivation and lack. My ever-shrewd brother, determined to escape into the night, hurriedly reads from the *Haggadah*. We quickly move on to taste the cold hard-boiled egg soup, before progressing to small pieces of fish. My brother excuses himself—"hey, Dickie's waiting"—and hastily exits to join his pals at their family events.

Why is this night different from all other Passover nights? Because I'm alone with Her that's why.

"God is watching you, you little bitch," my mother decrees as we finish the meal together. The refrain is all too familiar; nothing new or inspirational here. "Go on, you're just like your father. Godddddd will get you...."

I rush out the door, escape into my beloved Morris mini and head into the night. Almost by rote I drive to the plush Jewish enclaves where my cousins and other musicians live in great comfort. I seek their warmth. I park in front of the iron gates of the Muller family's house on Milton Street. I picture the gardens all alight, and in my mind's eye watch the willow tree lazing as usual over the deep pool. I envision a mammoth dining table balancing jugs of red wine and plates of chopped liver and chopped herring and dishes piled high with matzoh. Lights glow upstairs and I almost can feel the heat of the bodies close together in prayer and song.

I pull up outside the home of cousins Belle and Sol. I can practically taste their specialty: Danish herring in tomato sauce. Minutes away, down the hill, Uncle Louis' estate too echoes with frivolity.

I fill my insides with vicarious love and light and feel better. But a truth remains. Unlike the Israelites, I cannot escape my indenture, my servitude to a cruel and unrelenting Pharaoh. I have no place to go. She's waiting. Sitting on the bed in the room I must share with her. Night after Night.

"I knew you'd be back," my mother says, face flushing, as is her wont after her every triumph.

Aimless In Africa

Every morning I wake up and there you are. I awaken with electricity, a jolt, and an almost tangible feeling of creativity. But as my eyes open to the day, they adjust to reality. There you stand, all flushed before the dressing table with its three-sided mirror.

Readying for work, you brush your tinted brunette curls and paint your lips red before directing yet another meaningless non-sequitur my way: "Life," (pause and smack lips), "Life is the survival of the fittest." Or the hackneyed: "I command and demand respect," which you pronounce while parading the room in your panties.

I'm wasting my time here. I'm wasting my most glorious, fruitful, budding youth in the face of your unimagined life. You offer me no growth, no advancement into womanhood. Only your rantings.

I sometimes wonder how things would be had I been born to someone else? I wonder how different it might have been to wake up to, "Hello my darling daughter. Did you sleep well? Hello beautiful girl. I love you and am so proud of you. I am so lucky to have you."

Mostly I wonder how different life would look if my insides glowed with your praise?

Every day, everything appears the same. There are no new vistas, new skies, new people, new scenes or new customs appearing on my horizon. If I don't sit at the piano the entire day you deem me "slothful and lazy."

Sometimes I feel inspired, even reach lofty heights with Beethoven's glorious "Waldstein" sonata, especially the last movement. Other days I float when playing Ravel's ethereal *"Jeux d'eau."* Increasingly, though, my brain seems to be on autopilot. But I do manage to fool you, my taskmaster. After every hour of practice I settle into the blue-and-pink floral chair and for at least 20 minutes devour those Perry Mason mysteries. I think I've almost read them all.

As expected, I matriculate first-class, with history my ace subject. You appear *très* serious in your characteristic linen suit at the ceremony in the schoolyard where I'm awarded a volume of Shakespeare for best something or other. That's Friday afternoon. Monday morning you turn to me as I lay in bed, and while making your cheeks rosy with rouge recite what proves the mantra for my young life: "Get stuck in; get stuck in and practice ten hours a day." That's it; the only discussion we ever have about my future.

Kweekie, whom I increasingly regard as your lieutenant spy, brings me tea at 11 a.m., then joins me for lunch sitting on the edge-to-edge carpet in a spot of sunlight filtering through the glass patio door. We slurp down spaghetti with tomato sauce from a can, topping it all with grated cheddar cheese. Fridays, we share her native dish, dipping pieces of pap (mealie meal cooked in sour milk) into rich brown gravy. Sometimes we crown the lunch with grilled boerewors, that world-renowned delectable sausage spiced with ingredients so secret that only butchers dare guess their content.

Many afternoons, we hear the call of the African man as he lugs sacks of mealies (the Americans call these corn on the cob) up the hill: *"Hey, mealies, mealies, meallllleee, meallllleeeee,"* the street vendor cries in a weary crescendo. Each fetches him a shilling, if lucky.

You return afternoons from your lowly secretarial job at the Technical College downtown, often bearing gifts of teensy Nestlé chocolates to give me energy. You're also big on Cadbury bars at exam time and whenever under stress. In your view, the secret to being a successful assistant is anticipating the boss's every need, to the point of lining up pencils sharpened in perfect descending order. For all your efforts, you bring home about one-third of the earnings of men. You resent the stigma you believe you bear as a working woman. How you envy those rich trophy wives, whose lives revolve mostly around children, manicurists, hairdressers, bridge games and annoying lazy servants. You go on and on about the miseries of being employed. "Oh my suffering; I'm a woman aloooooooone."

Yet when Uncle Maish secures you a position as a medical secretary at the General Hospital where, as a radiologist he keeps rooms, you slowly appear, well, lighter, wearing the issued white hospital coat with pride, as if cloaking yourself in a newfound self-esteem. You opt to learn about nutrition and brag about eating a banana a day and taking baths in multi-minerals imported from Germany. You even exercise for the first time, walking several times down the road to the new supermarket Checker's, which stimulates with its variety of cheeses and breads and cheery conversations with anonymous clerks. There's been so little Down Here to excite. No television, and only in the late 1960s bars open doors to women. Suburban steakhouses spring up, and we start to frequent outlets for juicy, well-done burgers and onion rings.

I stop practicing around 5 or 6 p.m., and head for the library. I find a kind of sanctuary there, browsing shelves for autobiographies or British mysteries or American detective yarns. Most days I can hardly wait for Kweekie to return with the newspaper. Presumably, we're too poor to subscribe to a daily delivery; rather we buy our copies at the corner shop. I pore over every section of the evening Star, and spend hours scouring its arts coverage. Actually I relish comparing coverage between both dailies and the Sunday paper to see who does the best job, including book reviews. I'm not above calling an editor or a writer to point out lapses. What thrills me is that many listen to what I have to say. I also like entering contests, even sending along jokes, just as long as I get published. I once won a song contest. I like seeing my name in print. Top or bottom.

But these days you've concocted a new routine to disrupt my leisure time. You decide to take your bath in the late afternoon, *dafka* when I'm reading or dancing. You demand that exactly 20 minutes after you disturb me and announce your pending wash, I must come and keep you company and make sure you're ok.

"Why Mommy?
"I might die of a heart attack."

With a dread that permeates, I drop my book, or quit singing with Elvis on "I Wanna Be Free," and head for the bathroom. There you are, a silly scarf around your curls, splishing and splashing this way and that, washing yourself with your undies and yakking on and on. I sit on the wash basket alongside, smiling for my sanity as I indulge your inanities.

What a relief to finally be able to putter on the patio and read about classical music in my beloved magazine, Musical America. I can't get over the success of Van Cliburn. It's incredible that he won Moscow's Tchaikovsky Piano Competition. I love all those shots of him at a ticker-tape parade in New York. Oh God, I wish I could study in America.

I know how suspicious you remain of my attaining any real success beyond your narrow borders. That realization hits me in Technicolor during one supper conversation about cousins Lynnette and Hedy-Anne going on a trip to Europe, and regarding the future of that talented dancer Wendy who has won a scholarship to the Royal Ballet.

"You look so sad." For once, you actually observe my reaction. "Do you also want to go overseas?"
"Oh, I'd kill just to go to the Juilliard."
Silence. Incredulity.
"You mean you'd actually leave me?" Astonishment. Sans rancor.

I know then that I'm going nowhere.

SATURDAY NIGHTS

Around 6 p.m. each Saturday my mother checks the liquor cabinet for adequate scotch, soda, Kahlua, cognac and clean drinking glasses. Settling into a blue flowery lounge chair, she primps and prunes anticipating my date's arrival around 7.

Actually, preparations for this grand event have begun days earlier. By Monday afternoon, my mother has selected the clothes and underwear I must wear on my date. Shoes are polished, handbag touched up and a petticoat washed and pressed. The chosen outfit and matching accoutrements will hang the rest of the week outside the white bedroom wardrobe with the decorated gold scrolls.

I shudder as I walk past my skirt or dress or petticoat wafting in the breeze, gathering no doubt the freshness my mother believes men find so appealing.

Periodically, my mother with a solemn nanny standing alongside conducts wardrobe inspections. These can occur at any time. I barely conclude a run-through of Franz Schubert's ethereal Impromptu in A-flat when one such call comes.

"Dondela," my mother's affectionate call beckons. I walk into the room with a smile; I've finally achieved the *cantabile* in the bass line so desirous in the Schubert. Then I notice the opened drawers.

"You filthy little bitch," she starts, "look at your dirty petticoat. Did you think to ask Kweekie to wash it? And look at this hairbrush. All you have to do is give it to Kweekie. Isn't that right, Kweekie?"

"Ah, is true, Missie," her cohort acquiesces, adjusting her bra to accommodate those pendulous breasts.

I wish I could say I walk out in indignation or slam the bedroom door or head out to my beloved mini-mobile and drive away. But No; I do what I always do. Cry. "Leave me alone; you crazy woman." Snivel. Snot. She decides when to call it quits. Go and practice Dondela.

Mostly, my mother directs all efforts towards pleasing a man. On date night, she opens the door with a smile, plies my date with a drink and wishes us a happy night. If there's no date, she throws herself on the bed and proclaims Saturday night, "the lonnnnnnnneliest night of the week."

My mother has not touched the skin of a male since my Dad left when I was ten. From what I gather, she didn't touch him much either. When I later lived in Los Angeles, my father shared that he was made to wear not one, but two condoms. "She wouldn't even touch it," he expounded, as I hastened out the door.

Yet she readily dispenses tips to her budding daughter on "how to get" a man.
"Be warm," remains her favored directive. "Be a woman. Be warm; you're so cold."

Soon after she turned 81, my mother telephoned me in Los Angeles. She said she so hoped I had a boyfriend, someone to take me to a show. "But you must be warm," she reiterated, all the way from Africa. I almost fell off the bed. It was as if the hark of the lark had returned. I half-heartedly pointed out that not once in memory had she been with a man when she interrupted, saying an 88-year-old neighbor in her building fancied her. "I'm warm," she pointed out, "but of course it's too late now."

Decades earlier, she brazenly sets out to school her teen on the art of seduction. My mother's big on wilting. She suggests that after a date, when the car's parked and the engine switched-off for smooching, I grow weak and cast limpid eyes upon my prey. She advocates looking coy and fussing with a man's tie while on the dance floor. To convey the ultimate in helplessness, she urges feigning illness, but nothing too severe lest a potential suitor should flee in fear.

Saturday Night rules amongst the young Jews from Johies.
It's a time to be seen, preferably with someone good-looking
and with a good family pedigree. The city may seem a
sophisticated metropolis, but a highly judgmental, small
town mentality prevails. At the bio (movies) everybody knows
everybody and notices everybody. A newsreel from the BBC
usually precedes intermission. Before the main feature, our
date buys us a box of assorted chocolates, all individually
wrapped in foil, contents graphically displayed on lid. For
the less flush, there's vanilla or chocolate ice cream cups
with plastic spoons retrieved from ushers carrying trays.

In the 1950s and '60s, film features routinely are slashed
to eliminate full or even half-naked tits and bums. The
government-run censorship board has scant use for story
or plot lines.

Driving home with my date, panic sets in. If we park on the
street outside our flat, hungry eyes will be watching. As we
pull up, I see fingers pry open the Venetian blinds in the
bedroom. And should we opt to occupy the lounge sofa,
Her presence hovers just beyond the half-open passage
door. My mother demands I never close that door. "They'll
think I'm spying," she reiterates. I wish I'd asked my dates
to loudly declare: Oh Greta, I think I'll close the door.
Anything but do her bidding.

One midnight, after redhead Robbie Muller with the
freckles bids *bonne nuit*, having worked his magic one more

time, she pounces. "He touched your breast, he touched your breast." Eyes red. Cheeks flushed.

I discovered Randy Robbie on the beach in Durban where we spend annual vacations. I meet all my boyfriends there. Decembers, when South Africa starts shutting down for the Christmas break my mother dregs up enough money to take us to the coast by train. Able to afford only second-class we wait, in shame, in the green-and-brown compartment for the train to leave noisy Hillbrow station. Often, my beloved Auntie Fanny arrives to wave goodbye and slips my mother a few folded bills.

Minutes after departure, my mother demands I join her on bended knee:
"Please God let my Gitella meet a man," she prays. She started nagging God the year I turn 13. Soon she ups the ante, pleading that the man be rich.
"Please God let me meet a man," I may concur on my knees, but my tender teen heart begs otherwise.

When the conductor collects the tickets, my mother places our breakfast order. I climb a little ladder and fold into the top bunk. I love listening to the *"tara tarum; tara tarum,"* as the train clacks through the night, tracking the 400 miles from Transvaal through the Natal province. We're awakened at 6 by the tickaticka rattling of the compartment door. All neat in his matching navy waistcoat, the steward places a plate piled with melting buttered toast on the small table under the window. He raises two silver pots and from way up high blends hot milk and dark roasted coffee into two cups waiting on a silvery tray below.

The summer temperatures in Durban soar well over 100 degrees, Fahrenheit, with horrendous humidity. My mother relaxes in a deck chair beneath a shaded umbrella in her flouncy dress, sandals, and a white organza scarf that shields her from the sun and also hides her flabby arms. All cheery, she munches on lychees sold by the bunch by Indian vendors, or enjoys toasted cheese sandwiches or scones and crème and jam delivered with cups of tea from a beachside food stand.

Why doesn't she wear bathing attire or ever go in the ocean or for that matter swim? "The doctor says the cold water could kill me; I could have a heart attack," she responds. So she takes it easy in the sun. She has other plans for her daughter. Supplying me with plunging bathing suit, she offsets any hint of impropriety by covering my budding cleavage with a white lace handkerchief (I hate that little pink rosebud folded in one corner), and demands I scour the beach for boys. The requirements for snaring a man in Durban differ from the mainland. In Johannesburg, I need only secure a date for Saturdays; here, a nightly rendezvous is the order. But on both coasts one cardinal rule remains inviolate: If a boy/man asks me out, saying no is not an option.

A naïve teen, I'm far happier just hanging out, often with Mommy, staring out to sea. The sun stays merciless, the sands scalding. And although I swallow tablets to prevent sunburn, twice I'm taken to a local hospital. They apply vinegar treatments and baby-powder dustings for the blisters covering my back and shoulders. Annoyed, my mother refuses to stay with me. I lie alone face down on the cool sheets, blisters bared.

Soonest, I'm required to resume beach patrol. Preferably, I land a date by noon and before returning for lunch to the Empress Hotel across from the beach. But never mind, there's still the afternoon to go on duty.

I love our lunches of curry and rice and chutney and raisins and coconut condiments prepared by Durban's marvelous Indian chefs. Then siesta. At 3:30 p.m. sharp, my mother awakens me. "Doll up, dress up, go on doll up," she says, before encouraging me out the door. I roam the beach, rest coyly on the back wall or troll at an afternoon party.

On my rounds I talk to some really nice boys. With big breasts protruding through various halter tops, I catch the attention of one, Harold Gottlieb, a mature, slight 17-year-old with a moustache. Harold smells like no other. As I look at the group picture taken all those summers ago, I can still remember the pleasure of him, particularly the night in his hotel room. Suddenly he's on top of me, his wet lips on mine. "Do you know what I could do to you," he begins his black eyes boring into my terrified browns. Whatever it is, he decides not to do it, and lets me go. Instinct forbids me to talk to Her about it. Harold ignores me after that, and I can't understand why.

By six o'clock, Durban's blazing sun ceases its brutalizing and gentle breezes prevail. I sit with my mom on the soft, cooling sands, free at last from the pressures of seduction. She loves me to comb her hair, finding the gentle strokes soothing. And she enjoys telling stories, namely about Lucky brother Louis, the only child of the six siblings to receive a proper education, or the beautiful, self-involved sister Bessie, an apparent seductress what with her black wavy hair and piercing blue eyes. Sometimes talk turns to Hitler and the Holocaust and neighborly betrayals.

My mother recalls her father dying mysteriously on a mission to the Belgian Congo when she was tiny, and on occasion speaks of a violent stepfather who cared only that his biological children should eat, ignoring the hunger of the other step-six. I sense great pain when my mother recounts being placed, together with her sister Fanny, in an orphanage for two years. She often says to me, as if reassuring herself, "You know, any other mother in my position would put you in an orphanage. You children are so lucky." I merely nod knowing those moments too shall pass.

Dawdling at dusk near the lifesavers' station on Durban's North Beach, my mother reminisces about her romances as a slender young woman, telling me repeatedly how she could have married rich Benny Brown, a man in diamonds. "Now look at me…"

As light blends into growing darkness and young lovers stroll arm-in-arm along the seaside promenade or take their places at posh eateries where lobsters and crayfish have surrendered to their fates, my mother starts her wailing: "I'm a woman alone; only Goddddd knows my suffering." I head with my date for the waterfront to rock at clubs until dawn. The next day's manhunt seemingly hours away.

Purple Pleats

My mother buys all my clothes (whether I want or like them, or not), chooses all styles, determines all lengths and worst of all dresses me in her image. I measure petite, she puts me in medium. And always with a plunging neckline made safe with a brooch or a bit of Kleenex or a little white hanky.

I dread going shopping. She demands I parade up and down, in this shoe and that sandal, and this jersey and that skirt, and with this bag and those gloves, until she finds her right look. "God; what a body you have," she says, staring. "Men will go crazy for you." She experiments with the hem, some poor seamstress on her knees, following orders to the inch. "No, no, longer, longer." Then we test the makeshift hem with heels. Then we try the look without. Walk sideways, walk front ways; walk long ways, back ways.

For one particular party, my mom purchases from John Orr's downtown department store a pretty shiny purple dress with pleats. Here, the neckline's offset with a bit of white lace trim. In the dressing room we run the routine, me parading up and down and swaying and swishing this way and that. In a rare departure, this day I determine the appropriate hemline. For once, the dress is quickly pinned and in minutes we're done and on our way home.

Coursing down busy Joubert Street in my two-door Morris mini-minor, my mother without warning starts flailing and wailing: "The hem is too long; the hem's too longgggggggggggg."

Opening the passenger door, she jumps into traffic. I can only stare in my rear-view mirror. I'm terrified she'll be struck down while darting madly from lane to lane. Oh no. She's fine, and resumes cursing once back home.

Ralph Regrets

After spying Ralph on Durban's northern beach, I swear to my friends back home that he's a James Dean look-alike, what with those big blue eyes, button nose and a rose mouth. Age 22, he's annoyingly short though, with skinny brown legs and a head of curly hair bronzed by the brutal Natal sun.

A med student at the University of the Witwatersrand, Ralph's expected to graduate in two years. In my mother's view, this augurs well for matrimony because after he serves his internship, she'll be home free with her son-in-law, the rich doctor. I just like Ralph; like to sit on his towel on the beach. One steamy afternoon Ralph takes me to the docks to meet his father who manages a crew of workers. At 19, and buxom in a low-cut white lace blouse tucked into skimpy white shorts, I step over yards and yards of coil. Watching the dock hands, I place the ships into a background frame. The impression lasts, as does my love of harbor fronts.

Ralph and I park often at Durban's famed Blue Lagoon, a coastal outlet that proves ideal for young lovers and local fishermen alike. We also frequent drive-ins. Ralph remains content merely to lace fingers around my full breasts, wanting nothing more then. We've been dating about nine months when my mother takes him aside, speaks of marriage and urges him to specialize in surgery, where she insists he "could clean up." Ralph just nods. His rather genteel upbringing hardly has prepared him for such shenanigans.

Shortly after announcing our engagement, we attend a party given by my friend Sandra, the brilliant scholar who always placed top of the class at Barnato Park High. Purportedly coming from a politically progressive family, Sandra forbade those of us in her inner circle to join in singing the Afrikaner national anthem, "Die Stem," during school assembly.

This Saturday night we're boppin' to Little Richard's "Tutti Frutti" when suddenly the music dies. Sandra's mother announces the unimaginable: President John F. Kennedy has been shot. "I don't believe it," Ralph repeats. "It's not true."

We all stand at attention, crowding a little black portable radio.
Beep. Beep. BeepBeep. "This is an emergency bulletin of the BBC," a British voice begins. Breathless, 60 kids wait hands and hearts locked.

"Drive a Volkswagen today," the national advertisers hug their prime spot. "Get stuffed you buggers," a teenager fights back.
"President John Fitzgerald Kennedy has been killed." Screaming. Sighing. Crying.

"I don't believe it; there must be some mistake," was what my Ralph repeats. Then he hurrrrumphs, as is his habit. I want to strike him there and then for always being out of touch with reality. Especially my reality. But then how could he have known the price I was paying for our burgeoning love.

I agree to accompany my mother one last time on our annual Christmas pilgrimage to the seaside at Durban. One humid afternoon a blue aerogramme arrives from my fiancée. I'm excited to read Ralph's words of love and attraction. Then I see Her starved and sullen look. I must make a quick decision. If I go into the bathroom and leave the letter on the bedside table she'll read it; if I take it in with me, she'll curse and scream and accuse me of mistrusting her. In the end, I shred the paper. As the blue shards trickle into the trash, she loses it. I lose out too: I can't savor my lover's affections, and there's scarcely time to record them in my heart for a later secret visitation.

Our wedding near, my mother decides that money-lugging Uncle Louis should pay for the reception. He agrees, but opts for an afternoon tea. My mother demands that a fancy dinner/dance be held at the colorful Moulin Rouge Hotel. Naturally, my father, "the rotter" is nowhere in sight. The way things work out my Dad never meets Ralph.

I'm as slender as a pencil in a white satin gown on our marriage day, December 26, 1965. In Johannesburg, if you're Jewish and unmarried at age 21, you might as well shoot yourself. You're an over-the-hill spinster with little hope of redemption. I make the deadline by three days. My father deems it absurd that he has to sign permission for the marriage. "Couldn't you have waited until your birthday on the 29th?" he laments from Los Angeles. My mother thinks otherwise.

After exchanging vows at Berea Synagogue, Ralph with great gusto stamps the glass covered with cloth—I love this Jewish ritual—thus sealing our fates. I lean forward to kiss him and in what will prove a sign for our times, Ralph whispers, "We're not supposed to (kiss)." I just stare at him. But jubilantly we run back down the aisle to Mendelssohn's "Wedding March." Later that night at the Parktown Hotel neither of us seems sure what to do. I'm wearing what my mom has purchased for the grand occasion: a white satin negligee, with matching bolero, and oh, could you vomit, silver satin slippers, with little heels. We lie in bed and don't sleep. It occurs to me that I know nothing of my body; hell, I didn't even know where to find my vagina. Nor does Ralph. The next day, we return to my mother for lunch before flying to Cape Town to begin our honeymoon. He boasts to my mother, "Greta is a woman now," as if either of us knows what that means.

We stay at a beautiful hotel on the beach in upscale Clifton, courtesy of his parents. I remember at twilight going into the elegant dining room and partaking of a buffet of giant prawns and grilled Dover sole, and feeling close to my husband at our candlelit table overlooking the sea. My birthday's two days into the honeymoon. All cheery and expectant, I ask Ralph: Where's my present?

I didn't get you anything. I don't believe him and look under the bed. In the wardrobe. In his suitcase. I'm miserable anyway because of such sunburn. We'd taken a cable car up Table Mountain, and I'm red and hurting. Suddenly Ralph's on top of me. We both laugh. On the radio the Rolling Stones blare, "*Hey, You, Get Off of My Cloud.*" I join them, yelling louder with each refrain, "Get Off Of My Cloud." Turns out to be our sexual anthem.

Back in Joh'burg, I give my mother hell. "You should have educated me, about my body, about where my vagina is, I know nothing," I cry.
"Nobody knows where anything is," she answers, waving her hands. "Nobody knows these things."

I begin looking at myself in one of those hand-held vanity mirrors that never quite refract the light where you want. Who in their right mind would devise such an anatomy? It mystifies me for years. I recall my shock at viewing artist Georgia O'Keeffe's flowers, and my incredulity when later confronted with Judy Chicago's multimedia "The Dinner Party." Let alone Eve Ensler's extraordinary theater piece, "The Vagina Monologues."

(But I long have been numbed against any such awakening. Weeks prior to my marriage my mother arranges that I be hospitalized and my hymen stretched under anesthesia, a local custom, she insists, and supposedly befitting all virginal Jewish brides-to-be. Days after my discharge, I develop a horrible pain and have to plead with an obviously inconvenienced brother, accompanied by my equally irritated mother, to drive me to the outpatient center where my gynecologist awaits. I've developed an infection and he prescribes antibiotics, which he probably should have done in the first instant. I remember walking back to the car, feeling the shame between my legs.)

With Ralph graduated and earning some pittance, we move into Resdoc, a facility for married interns situated near the Johannesburg General Hospital. We occupy two rooms, one with a basin and a shared bathroom down the hall. I love it when Ralph comes around faithfully each morning as I sleep and kisses me bye before going to the hospital. I love walking by his naked chest and chatting while he shaves in the mirror. I love dressing up and going dancing or to the movies. I love walking, holding hands, or sitting together on a park bench or going to the Doll's House drive-through for hamburgers and cokes.

I just live in dread of the nights. Spent together. In bed. The only time I allow myself to flirt fully and become amorous is when I have my period. When I feel safe from intrusion. Now, I weep for those wasted nights, especially when I remember Ralph's response to my suggestion that making love to a recording of Beethoven's Fourth Piano Concerto might just do the trick (I find the sequential crescendos in the first movement quite orgasmic). Ralph came home that very day with a Deutsche Grammophon recording. I can still see the yellow label spinning on the little gray turntable on the ledge above our bed.

Idiot that I am, I resume my practice daily on the black grand piano located at my mother's flat. As afternoons draw to a close, my mom prays, hands clasped, at the window: "Oh, God, please God, give me my baby back. I want my baby back." She phones me at Resdoc, sometimes ten calls an evening. It reaches the point where I dial her, literally reporting when Ralph enters or exits our quarters.

At times, we newlyweds do strive for autonomy; if we hadn't been fooled back into the fold, we may well have survived. Poor Ralph, depleted from nightly intern duty, opts one Sunday for a rare picnic. We anticipate resting in each other's arms. I accept my mother's offer of a hamper of roasted chicken and salad and arrive at her flat, all smiles. Again, she's at her bedroom window.

"I'm so excited, my husband and I are off to the park," I greet her. Face flushed, she turns and with a look of pure vitriol: "Hmmmmm, you little bitch, you said 'husband.' You're rubbing it in because I don't have one, aren't you?" I feel drained, and ultimately, make miserable my Sunday in the Park with Ralph.

Our chances for unity fade further when months into the marriage I compete in an international piano contest in Italy. My program for the Alfredo Casella Competition in Naples ranks a short piece by the namesake Italian composer, as well as Liszt's "Tarantella," and works by Bach and Haydn. And for the concerto portion, Ravel's wonderfully jazzy G Major, in three movements. Six weeks before my trip, my mother invites the music critic from the Rand Daily Mail to hear me play in a private setting. Mrs. Sowden, later named dance critic at the Jerusalem Post, comes willingly to the Upper Houghton home of a rich friend (my mother shrewdly arranges my appearances in plush surroundings away from the confines of our flat). The scribe for the morning paper enjoys a cup of tea from a delicate floral cup, before listening to my recital on a Steinway. She offers some suggestions, and the next day runs an article pleading my case and announcing my forthcoming benefit appearance at Bobolink, the Sandhurst home of wealthy arts patrons, Mr. and Mrs. R.N. Harvey.

"*Undaunted, fine young pianist needs help,*" the Rand Daily Mail declares 3/3/1966:

> "*When I first heard Greta Beigel play, she was a pretty little girl of 10, with a mother rather anxious to know what to do with such a precocious pianist. She is now a lovely young newlywed and a pianist so fine that she goes to Italy for an international competition, with a sporting chance of winning...* "

Saturday night I wait in a room adjoining the Harveys' concert lounge for the performance to begin at 8. My brother's nowhere to be seen. But matriarch and spouse are at it:

"You have noooohhhh right to be here," my mother informs the pacing Ralph.

"I have every right, I am her husband," Ralph protests.

I just shake. At the best of times, I'm not partial to playing before people who for space reasons or sold-out events crowd the piano. I prefer to remain aloof up high. Throughout the Liszt, my right knee knocks so hard I hardly can control the pedal.

"One has always known Greta Beigel's technique to be assured," the Star comments the next night. *"That she was able to manage the pyrotechnics of the Liszt 'Tarantella' from 'Venezia* e *Napoli' was no surprise. What matters, is that this is now combined with more serious musicianship and a deeper vision."*

The review in the morning daily is more on target, excusing all by reporting that I was nervous. Later, a clerk at Teddy Bear's Fisheries (and groceries) compliments me, but word had gotten around, she says, that I was very jittery. Talk about feeling mortified.

Then the crucial ten days before I leave for Italy. That week, my mother concludes that I'm so rotten I can no longer come over to practice. I plead, to no avail. Strangely, Ralph and I bond in our joint dilemma and disbelief. Standing one morning outside Resdoc's kitchen—if you popped in there, cockroaches scattered left and right—Ralph assures me not to worry. "I'll get you a piano, I'll buy you one." I relax in his arms; I do believe I actually flirted "Oh will you Ralph?" Dummy, I immediately relay Ralph's pending generosity to my mother.

"I didn't mean it," her voice syrupy, both eyes twitching. "Of course you can come and practice. Don't bother Ralph. He doesn't need to buy you a piano."
Oh, Ralph, if only you had.

My mom contacts the Rabbi of Naples to meet me and make sure I reach my hotel safely. Once unpacked, from the chilly room I dial Ralph at Resdoc to say hello. He's cold and detached in a barely audible way. En route to the concert auditorium, I jump on the streetcar, praying silently for an accident so that I could lose an arm so that I won't have to practice anymore. I'm all of 21. So grateful not all of our prayers are answered.

The friendly rabbi, a small man with a huge beard remains busy on my behalf. Straight-faced, he arranges for me to practice at the home of a member of the competition jury. He also buys me, a kosher girl, a cheeseburger, and takes pleasure watching my every bite. He deems it disgraceful though that I wear lipstick.

I fail to advance beyond the first round. I'm now freed to enjoy the contest and goof off with other participants. I spend a glorious afternoon in the baking sun at the ruins of Pompeii, relaxing on the grass with a German pianist and a new friend, Supitra Riensuvarn, an exquisite 18-year-old musician from Thailand, who later presents me with a stopwatch metronome. We don't speak the same tongue, but understand each other's limited French forays just fine. Especially when expressing our sentiments over the rumored rigging of the proceedings in favor of a local Neapolitan boy.

Mostly, I'm deeply moved by the tonal qualities of a young pony-tailed pianist from California, one Gabriel Chodos. He's a student in Los Angeles of pedagogue Aube Tzerko, himself a student of Artur Schnabel. (Chodos goes on to an established career, teaching at Boston's New England Conservatory of Music.) Immediately upon returning to South Africa, I scrawl Tzerko's name in purple crayon inside the wardrobe door at my mom's flat. It proves fortuitous.

A grumpy Ralph meets me at Jan Smuts Airport. Instead of driving to our residence—I actually want to hug, even make out—to my annoyance he proceeds, almost by rote, to my mother's flat. "Let's go home first," I say. "No, we have to go there; she's waiting." And there she lies, propped up by pillows, apparently having been deathly ill. Relatives, namely Auntie Bessie, Auntie Gertie and my cousin Belle, surround her. They all cluck cluck; Ralph sulks. And we both feel like losers.

Resdoc routines continue: Communal meals, afternoon teas, Saturday night socials and always the passage of exhausted, overworked interns. Ralph often returns at 4 a.m., mostly drained, but sometimes full of giggles. In particular he can hardly contain himself when recounting the travails of a female patient whose jaw had locked under very suspicious circumstances. I'm not overly appreciative.

There exists an unstated code among doctors in South Africa. They agree to medically treat each other and their respective families, gratis, should the need arise. Apparently, that courtesy also extends to cosmetics.

Getting a nose job can be highly prized. My mother, who has the loooooongest nose, sees no need to change her condition. After all, her brothers and sisters all are blessed with large proboscises. However, she's desperate and determined to improve my look.

She contacts Dr. Penn, the big nose man in South Africa. He agrees to sculpt me at no cost to my doctor husband. Dr. Penn begins our initial consultation by screaming. Apparently my mother-in-law Hilda, who hates my mother almost as much as my mother detests her, has called the office saying that the marriage's no good and that my mother's merely trying to get a freebie. I start crying and Dr. Penn caves.

After the operation, I'm wheeled to a general ward at the Brenthurst Clinic that I share with three other women. No husband, no mother in sight. Heavily sedated, I literally fall off the narrow bed and a patient yells for help. It's hell. I wear a giant Kotex pad under my ever-bleeding and swollen nose through which I can't breathe; that blood soon fills my mouth through which I can't breathe. Three days later still not one visitor. I finally call my mother. Annoyed, she arrives by taxi and drops me off at the doctors' residence. I can't remember Ralph's reaction.

Bruised and battered, the bandages come off two weeks later. No difference. Still a big nose. Furious, my mother prevails upon Dr. Penn to do a second job. Back I go for another bashing. But this time, I'm mildly inconvenienced and yes, three weeks later there appears something new. Strangely, the remodeling renders me looking more like my Dad.

At Resdoc, wives dutifully remain weekends with their doctor hubbies on call. Not me. I simply bugger off with friends, or go practice or hang out with Mommy. My most egregious failing, not only as a companion but also as a human being remains how I treat Ralph when he learns by phone call of his father's death in a freak accident. Owner and supervisor of a large complex of beachside flats in Durban, his Dad had jumped to his death when an elevator stalled. Feeling claustrophobic, he pried open the door and leapt. With Ralph crying, and me in what I can now only conclude in robotic mode, I head out to my scheduled piano lesson.

"Don't you think you should be with your husband?" my teacher suggests softly. I'm a sport though. I fly to Durban for the funeral. I catch cold by this time and lie in bed, groaning for a doctor. "You're not the only person who counts here you know," Ralph's mother, Hilda, chides. The doctor eventually arrives, and despite my admonitions that both parents were allergic to penicillin, he gives me a shot in the thigh. The telltale rash soon appears.

In recent years I've reached out to Ralph. First, I sent him a note of apology written on pink paper in a pink envelope addressed to the famed Houston hospital where for many years he has served as oncologist-gynecologist, doing so well that his work has been recognized by President Clinton. Months pass, and receiving no response, I leave a phone message.

I've just returned from lunch to my desk at the Los Angeles Times—did I tell you I'm a staff writer and arts editor there?—when the phone rings.
"This is Ralph."
I can hardly breathe. "Is this Dr. Ralph, I mean the real Dr. Ralph?" I joke. "Yes."

The line has developed one of those awful long distance echoes and I must hear everything I say twice. My luck, this day two film critics are in the newsroom, filing reviews at their pods on either side of me. But I'm afraid to hang up. And miss him again.

Yes he received my pink letter. He's remarried and has two children. Ralph also expresses concern about the ravages of age on his body. I must say this cheers me no end. I tell Ralph how sorry I am for so much and he says: "There is no need to say you are sorry; we were both so young."

I can still picture that Monday morning, all those years ago when Ralph left for the hospital and I took down the gray stereo turntable from the closet and—I can barely type the words—moved back to mother. To be fair, there were signs

predicting the split. For weeks while on the bed chatting, or getting dressed, I'd howl at Ralph the Nancy Sinatra hit refrain:
These boots are made for walkin' and that's just what they'll do
*One of these days these boots are gonna...*Or something like that.

Ralph's final admonition at the end of our ridiculous union that lasted less than a year remains emblazoned in memory: "If you fail at this marriage you will never marry again." In the divorce settlement I keep my father's $500 gift; Ralph receives the canteen of cutlery his uncle had sent us. The Supreme Court issues the final decree in Johannesburg on Dec. 21, 1966.

According to Jewish law, however, no marriage is dissolved until a document of divorce known as "*get*" is exchanged between the about-to-be-exes. And while Reform rabbis have accepted a civil decree in the event of remarriage, many American rabbis, as well as the Israeli rabbinate refuse to officiate should either party have divorced without securing a *get*. Decades-in-and-decades-out around the Diaspora, the issue remains volatile, hostile, with requirements and procedures for getting a *get* in a constant state of flux.

In South Africa in the 1960s, the *get* remains highly-prized by young Jewish women seeking to terminate a marriage. Stories abound about local bad boys notorious for demanding huge amounts before agreeing to the release. But there's no dispute that we'll both go and get the *get*. Ralph stops by the synagogue and reads biblical texts before the rabbi. I follow separately, clothed in the same light blue button-down dress and stupid matching hat that I wore to the civil proceedings. At that court, I developed a nervous twitch and no doubt in an apparent misunderstanding of my dilemma, Judge Ludorf winked back at me.

This time, the rabbi and various officers of the Jewish Ecclesiastical Court encircle me, spit at me, a woman obviously defiled. I go into a kind of shock, and stay away from synagogue for many years to come. "It sounds as if what happened to you, happened in a *shtetl*," commented an official from one New York-based non-profit that helps women who must contend with recalcitrant spouses. "Abuses are mainly to extort money. Your case is idiosyncratic."

Two years after the divorce my brother accompanies me to the American Consulate in downtown Johannesburg. Head down, he suddenly mutters: "Don't look now, but there's Ralph."(Once a man's on the outs my mother mandates that nobody mentions his name, let alone greets the bastard.)

I jump up and speak to Ralph who's applying for a visa. Even now I remember the closeness of our meeting.

I wish I could stand and breathe next to him just one more time.

ONE-MOVEMENT GAL

For decades, the Johannesburg Symphony has helped foster young artists by hosting concerto evenings at the University of the Witwatersrand. The prized programs feature six instrumentalists each performing but one movement from a concerto.

Sunday morning auditions take place at the studios of the South African Broadcasting Corporation (S.A.B.C.). Oh, what joy for our family when conductor Jeremy Schulman phones during lunch to say I've been chosen to play the Beethoven Third (3rd movement). Another time he accepts the Liszt E-flat (a complete work, in one long swoop). Then the Saint-Saëns' Second (first movement), and another all-in-one showstopper, Weber's glitzy Concertstück. (My repertory also includes the Schumann concerto and the Ravel G Major.)

Following my performance of the fleeting finale of the Beethoven Third at the Great Hall, my mother meets Gerda, a sort of family friend, in the lobby.

"What do you think?" Waiting. Breathless.
"Well, it was over, so fast," the world according to Gerda. My mother's eye twitches. "Hmmm. Too quick huh?"

Following any concert there's a lull what with all the preparation and excitement. But a less than sensational review or appraisal such as Gerda's sends our entire household into a mandatory, collective depression lasting days or weeks, or as long as my mother prescribes. When she recovers, I'm expected, once more, "to get stuck in and get on with it."

At age 19, I play the Liszt No. 1 with the Johannesburg Symphony and then later in Durban. The reviews register a mix.

".... Of the four pianists Greta Beigel was quite the most seasoned and dexterous in the Liszt, and clearly has the makings of a concert performer of artistry and skill," the much-dreaded critic Oliver Walker comments in the Star.

"Most polished playing came from Greta Beigel, 19," Dora Sowden writes in the Rand Daily Mail. *"She gave an amazing performance of the 'Triangle' concerto-she should not have chosen Liszt. One can understand a young pianist endowed with fast fingers and a strong sentiment wanting to pit her powers against this granite. But a slip of a girl is just*

*not built for it. If a woman plays this work at all, it must be a
Bachauer...Had she chosen Chopin or Schumann there need
perhaps have been no 'but' in my 'bravo.'"*

(I know a few who'd give her butt a bravo alright for suggesting
that only big-built pianists can bag the big works.)

For one spring appearance I prepare the opening movement
of the Saint-Saëns No. 2. I know the work intimately; it
positively sparkles in my hands. About three weeks before
the event, my mother invites a sometimes friend of hers
to join us in a rented practice room and run through the
orchestral part so I might familiarize myself more fully
with the *tuttis* and my entrances.

Hannah R., a slender brunette in her 30s, often plays
second piano at local eisteddfods and rehearsals. My
mother regales with stories of how Hannah's father, a
Russian brute, was partial to putting a boot to his wife's face
as his terrified little girl looked on. She mocks Hannah's
husband, the rosy-cheeked Harold who remains supportive
of his wife's artistic yearnings. They both like my mother.

We meet downtown, and I run through the Saint-Saëns.
My tempo remains propulsive, my mood playful. Hannah
has her take. She wants a slower speed here and a delaying
tactic there. It's Plod-along-Cassidy all the way, and I want
none of it.

"Who do you think you are?" my mother sneers, leaning
her heavy frame over the music stand, blue linen suit

rubbing against shiny black Steinway. I grab my score and handbag and run out the room, out the building, and into busy Eloff Street, a major artery throughout the city center. Mile after mile I flee, tears mingling with the breeze. I'm outside the block of flats where German-born Mrs. Wild lives and teaches. I want to cry to her, and imagine her saying: "This is crazy; you are my student, and we know what we are doing. Why are you even playing for somebody else? Why does your interpretation not count? Who is this woman Hannah and what does she know anyway?" But I fear the look on her face should I disturb her in the middle of a lesson. I shrug, give up and take a bus home.

An hour later, my mother knocks on the front door. "I knew you'd be here," she says looking more relieved than triumphant. "Where else would you go?"

But mostly it's the frilly, trilly Weber Concertstück that lodges in my brain, tormenting me long after I cease performing the work. Recorded with great panache by Austrian pianist Friedrich Gulda, this trite work/ballad tells of love lost and then found. About midway, there's one hellava glissando leading to a series of frivolous keyboard flourishes and trumpet turns, all signaling the return of our hero who has gone off to fight in the Crusade.

"The music moves with elegance and verve, and Miss Beigel captured a good deal of the spirit of it in a very clearly articulated performance," the morning critic wrote of my appearance with the Durban Municipal Orchestra at City Hall.

Soon I'm offered a lunch-hour concert to record the Weber with the S.A.B.C. Symphony Orchestra before an invited audience. At the first rehearsal, conductor Anton Hartmann makes his position clear.

"If you keep rushing and don't follow my rhythm, I will cancel your concert Miss Beigel. Do you understand?"

Looking as though she's received a death notice my mother retreats behind her bedroom door, and for the first time in my entire life, leaves me alone to work. For the first time, I'm fully present when I practice; at one with the music before me. Through gritted determination, I articulate every note according to a metronome beat, slowly, surely, building up a solid, defining rhythm.

When the downbeat comes the next day at rehearsal, I'm in charge and alert, and the orchestra players give me a foot-stamping cheer.

But I'm soooo tired. Mommy suggests we go away for a weekend to a local resort not too far from Johannesburg called Santa Barbara. En route, my beloved car hits an embankment and I'm afraid the radiator might blow. My mother keeps on talking as though it's the norm for two people to swerve off the road and become stuck in a ditch.

We settle into our bungalow and my mom puts on a white blouse and adjusts a striped skirt over her hefty hips.

Seems supper's a communal affair. We share a table with two couples that talk amongst themselves. We're ignored.

Walking back in the dark, my mother stumbles over a rock on the dirt path.

"Couldn't you have helped 'a' mother" she turns to me. "You bit of rubbish you. God is watching..." We enter the cottage. Red-faced, she pulls up her bed sheet, screaming, cursing and never missing a beat. Whatever exhaustion had brought me to this place now weighs heavily; I feel as if I'm attached to a rope being pulled down by a very large stone. The next morning she tells me I'm killing her, "You're putting me in my graaaaave."

But she does so enjoy listening to the radio broadcast of my taped performance that airs a few weeks later. I do too. It's a thrill and I don't sound too bad, except for the wrong notes.

The ensuing nightmares surrounding the Weber take years to subside. In these virtual images, I'm playing the back-and-forth C-major arpeggios, followed by chromatic flourishes found in the recapitulation of the Weber. Some nights I hit the right notes; other times I fluff 'em. I wake up drenched, but soon return to calm, ever-grateful in the knowledge that I never ever have to play those passages again as long as I shall live.

Prelude

I'm sunning myself on a bench on our balcony back home. Don't the geraniums in the brick beds look nice? And I love this rock magazine from America. My mother appears suddenly, enunciating an astonishing demand: "Write to Richard in America and ask for money."

Whaaaaat! We've never been allowed to utter Daddy's name since the divorce (only she's permitted to curse him out daily). Now I should write?

Dutifully I comply and receive sweet letters from Los Angeles in return. Mainly, Daddy expresses concerns over my music. Why so much time at the keyboard? Where's it all going?

I'm hardly making a living from concertizing although I do bring in regular monies teaching Jewish kids in wealthy suburbia. Of course, I immediately hand over all earnings to my mother. She awakens me Sundays at 9 with a breakfast of eggs and toast for stamina until I finish teaching four hours later. After a hectic Saturday night out, it's all the more torture. Teaching kids theory and how to read music remains a real drag; mostly I feel inadequate. But I enjoy the fancy teas at fancy houses.

The Muller family—all buddies with Uncle Louis—remains my fave. Lily Muller considered thee Joh'burg beauty what with those icy blue eyes remains sociable and generous, serving me lovely scones and cakes and paying me on time for teaching her children. After lessons, she often walks me around lush garden landscaping to view her latest plantings. The Muller compound contrasts sharply to the deprivation and growing dangers of my home environment.

To my mother's concern—you could say shock—my brother recently has met a dark-haired woman with a long nose and an ugly temper. Her father ranks "filthy" rich, and apparently approves my brother's commitment to financially take care of my mother, forever. He even agrees to wipe out his future son-in-law's existing debts.

Mary dare not openly convey her deep displeasure at the pending nuptials. Better to confront me with a virtual wall of hostility. I become fearful that she'll attack me with a knife, and make close friend Phyllis promise that should her phone ring in the dead of night and no one be at the other end, she'll come running. "I will Gret."

I must escape Africa. I must. My only hope lies in winning a music scholarship to study abroad; that way she wouldn't dare stop me from leaving. I've long ceased caring whether I'll ever make it to the Juilliard or Curtis, or for that matter the Royal Academy in London. Winning means my ticket out.

I turn to the Pretoria Govt.-funded University of South Africa (UNISA) regarding their prestigious annual overseas scholarship. I'm ruled eligible to compete, but first need to pass an exam in general musicianship as well as sit for my Performers Licentiate in Music.

In a few short months, I cram in at least six years of study in harmony, counterpoint, form and history with the affable Mr. Cherry, who instructs me Saturday mornings at the dimly-lit desk in his modest home. Far from a trendsetter in the music community, Mr. Cherry wears round spectacles and worn-out clothes made even more grungy by the massive ash droppings from the pipe he smokes non-stop. With fingers stained from constantly dipping a worn ivory quill into a scrubby little inkwell, he corrects my manuscripts, or scrawls brief histories about composers or in detail describes the salient qualities of each orchestral instrument. With him, I feel transported to an earlier era, where the great eccentric music masters prevailed.

Lucky for me, our work together caters mostly to my left brain, dictated by harmonic and melodic rules and constraints that I readily comprehend. As a result, I fare reasonably well at the exam, scoring enough to pass and move forward. But the day the Licentiate piano exam dawns I have a high fever. No doubt it's the flu. Seated at the Steinway before five staring adjudicators in this otherwise empty space in Pretoria, I barely run through those stupid, requisite scales and arpeggios.

"Please do C-sharp major ascending in the right hand; how about B-flat descending in the left? And let's see what you can do with B melodic minor both hands ascending and descending," one juror demands.

My playing of Bach's Partita No. 1 sounds even and fair; a normally-bravado set of variations by Glazunov passable. But there's nothing here to set the auditorium on fire. To be eligible for the scholarship, participants have to achieve a score of 175 out of 200. To the mortification of my teacher, piano guru Adolph Hallis—I hardly hold him in high regard anyway—I scrape by at 169.

There and then I promptly announce my retirement. Surprisingly calm, my mother lets me completely be. For three weeks I do no work. I relax for hours on the balcony reading American music magazines and pulp. Sometimes I meet friends at the bioscope or hang out looking for boys at Yeoville's public swimming pool nearby. I get a heavy taste of normal and like it.

Mesmerized by one famous shoot of a sulky Elvis sprawled on a train bunk surrounded by fan mail, I feel the longing for America grow ever-stronger in my young loins. Nanny

Kweekie interrupts one reverie. Madam's on the phone from work.

"Get stuck in," my mother declares at her most dramatic. "You're being allowed to compete for the prize. Get stuck in and practice 10 hours a day." I never find out why I've been accepted. My mother reasons that my outstanding reputation has cleared the path. I suspect she worked her tragic Jewish mother routine brilliantly.

Something changes inside of me. I practice far less than 10 hours, and my playing remains taut and rhythmic; my interpretations secure and sound. I assume a "don't mess with me" attitude; this contest constitutes life or death.

Five finalists each play a recital program on Tuesday morning. "I was terrific," I tell a relieved Mr. Hallis. But we hit a snag. There's to be a public performance in Pretoria on Friday night; at the conclusion, the winner announced. Trouble is the event will take place *erev* Yom Kippur, the holiest date on the Jewish calendar. I don't do anything then, other than recline and/or worship. I decline to appear. Mr. Hallis gnashes his teeth in despair, as he does at the best of times. The chairman of the committee calls. An Afrikaner, he remains sympathetic to my plight. "We are a religious lot," he explains to my receptive teacher, who considers this sudden empathy a good sign.

Mr. Hallis arranges for a student to attend the final Friday concert, and no matter what the hour to phone in the results.

At 6:30 Friday evening, Mother Mary places a pair of candles in decorated silver holders. The night is doubly holy, given that Yom Kippur has fallen on the Sabbath. Covering her head with a white lace shawl and making circular hand motions, she says the blessing for lighting the candles. Without missing a beat, she turns to me, demanding that I try on a pair of orange sandals she had purchased earlier in the day and without my knowledge.

I tell her I'm very nervous about the scholarship this night. I have a lot on my mind and will try on the sandals another time. She pinches hard; it has to be done now. I must parade from the table to the couch, and back again. "Walk to the liquor cabinet; walk to the piano." Left and right and backwards and forwards click the sandals. "I need to see how they look when the strap is tightened." She puts the clasp through the first hole. "Walk up; walk down." Now let's see how things look when we tighten the second hole.

"Enough, I can't take any more," I scream. Eyes growing alarmingly larger, my mother starts to moan in a scary crescendo, then yanks and breaks a sandal strap. "You rotten little bitch..grrrrrr." She's off and running for an hour. Eventually as is her custom, she puts herself to bed.

It's only 8 o'clock. Shit, I have to wait until midnight for the news. Sitting alone on a blue flowery chair, I feel a glorious sense of possibility stirring, growing, glowing......

At 1 a.m. the phone rings.

"You got it. You got it Greta," Mr. Hallis yells. I wish I'd taken some sheets from the passage closet and made up a simple bed in the lounge and left my mother to wonder what had happened, or merely driven off someplace. Instead I go in to tell this suffering soul in bed the good news. She hops right out, bright and full of vim, and then we go through one of the standard routines following every one of her cycles.

"Say you're sorry to 'a' mother," she instructs. I must hug her. She declares her forgiveness. Despite the hour, she starts phoning the world.

The next morning we send flowers to Mr. Hallis, and my mother contacts every journalist she knows; soon members of the English, Jewish and Afrikaans press arrive. Actually since age 7, and certainly after every triumph, my mother has schlepped me to the various newsrooms. I've grown comfortable in that milieu. I believe I belong there.

A few weeks pass and I record a recital of my scholarship program at the studios of the S.A.B.C. The engineer agrees to make an extra tape. I send that copy to famed piano pedagogue Aube Tzerko, a UCLA professor and former student of Artur Schnabel, whom I first heard about at an international piano competition in Napoli. He accepts me as a student. The way fate presents it, my father now resides in West Hollywood, a mere 20 minutes' drive from Tzerko's home in the Hollywood Hills. Daddy agrees to forward me a plane ticket to the States.

"Greta Beigel to Study in Hollywood," the Jewish Times reports on March 8, 1968.
"Tape Recording is Key to Future," the headline reads in the Rand Daily Mail.

I still possess the clip of the photo in that morning daily of me sitting cross-legged on top, yes on top, of my piano, sensually running the tape spool through my hands. I'm wearing the orange sandals that my mother had wrought.

DIAMONDS AND RUST

A friend who married and moved to the diamond town of Kimberley invites me to play a farewell recital as a fundraiser for her Jewish women's group. I unpack my bags at Glenda's home, and head for the art gallery where my program of works by Bach, Glazunov, Casella and Liszt is slotted for 8 p.m.

Without a dressing room, I wait in a car parked outside. I believe in grand entrances and will not be seen in a hall either before or after a concert. Alone, and all dressed up in a mauve flowered skirt and sequined matching top, I suddenly start shaking. This has never happened, although in recent weeks I've broken out in blisters on both hands; one doctor prescribes cortisone, another feeling something more is at stake, suggests we talk and offers Valium.

I barely get through the program, and hardly believe the applause, let alone that an encore, "The Juggler" by

Ernest Toch, is warranted. The next day's headline is kind: *"Youthful Pianist has a Wealth of Talent,"* proclaims reviewer W.W.

At a cheese and wine reception in my honor—I stand a seductive waif in a black low-slung crepe number—I make myself a silent promise.

"You never ever have to go through this again, Greta." (Wish I could stop the shaking.) "You never have to play again."

I Want To Be In America

"Remember," my brother administers as I prepare to board a plane for London, "things can't get any worse; they can only go up from here."

Only days before, I'd attended my brother's wedding. All blonde and emaciated in a blue-sequined gown I'm captured in a lovely photo dancing with the beaming groom. His face looks all greasy.

Now, as my TWA flight approaches Los Angeles, my brother's words of encouragement resonate. Suddenly the man next to me points: "Look, look at the lights as we land; you'll never see a display like this anywhere else." He's right; but what's it going to be like staying with my father?

There's Daddy! That's him. That little man with the furrowed brow and parted silvery hair pacing the gate at LAX. Spying me, his skinny daughter with a left eye that doesn't stop twitching whom he hasn't seen in nearly 14 years he slaps a ruddy cheek: "Oi vai, what have they done to you?"

Accompanied by a Russian relative, he takes me for my first meal to Bob's Big Boy in Toluca Lake. I gobble down a double cheeseburger. Having grown up strictly kosher, where milk and meat never mix, I've never tasted anything as mushy or magnificent as two meat patties smothered in cheese and something called Thousand Island dressing.

A few more treats await. Accustomed to munching salads of simply washed lettuce and tomatoes, now I discover creamy dressings. Also yogurt mixed with fruit, and the strangest of all, the bottomless cup of coffee, each refill plied with some weird rich dairy product called Half-&-Half. The best surprise comes on a later visit to distant relatives in Rochester, N.Y. where I'm given a peanut butter sandwich smothered in of all things, a sticky marshmallow spread. Talk about ecstatic. In the first nine months, I gain 15 pounds.

I also discover television and promptly abandon reading. I love Saturday mornings with my father in our West Hollywood apartment. He eases himself into the brown leather adjustable chair and together we watch old Edward G. Robinson movies. "Cookela, this is the greatest actor," my Dad insists. He also adores singer Mario Lanza's movies and worships the voice of tenor Enrico Caruso. My dad often sings along to the recordings of the great arias, insisting my musicality comes from his side of things.

Strictly a loner, he counts no friends in America. But Saturday nights we both venture out, me on a date with some guy I find at a Jewish singles dance; my Dad, in baggy pants and a cardigan, finds a kind of refuge up the hill at the Pussycat Theater on Santa Monica Blvd. I'm happy, because he's happy.

Our apartment complex increasingly attracts Russian immigrants who walk to Fairfax Boulevard nearby, that bustling artery lined with Jewish bookstores and bakeries and fisheries and delis and kosher eateries.

Friday afternoons, my father calls from the liquor store where he works part-time and invites me to join him for dinner, either at Argo's corner coffee shop or at Canter's 24-hour deli on Fairfax. He rarely reneges, no matter how much his feet hurt, or if there's been a hold-up at the store, something that happens with alarming frequency. Although he refuses to elaborate, Daddy was held at gunpoint during one robbery.

At Argo's we enjoy chopped steaks followed by Jell-O. My Dad gulps down his meal in 20-minutes flat. Canter's demands more attention. The smell of fresh pickles assaults the senses upon entry, while the bakery beckons with bear claws and the prune, pineapple, or cherry Danish that my father so relishes. Counters to the right boast of turkey, chopped liver, beef brisket, tongue, pepper beef, wine, crackers and assorted mustards.

My father eschews red vinyl booths in favor of the central dining room where we order complete dinners, ranging then from $8-12. We contemplate roast brisket of beef with potato pancake, or broiled beef liver or my Dad's favorite, broiled hamburger steak and sautéed onions. Appetizers include chopped liver, for me, and salted herring for the boss. Often he partakes of borscht with cream, while I have my matzo ball soup with rice. And of course piles of fresh rye.

Returning home, my father grimaces as he takes off his shoes. He worries a lot about resting his legs. He fears cramping and sits in his armchair for long periods, especially when preparing for nightly stints on his feet serving customers.

My Dad obsesses over three entities: money, his tired legs and bowel movements. The latter's the easiest to ignore; I just roll my eyes at his descriptions. But his penurious practices prove the hardest to endure. Shortly after my arrival, my father comes charging into my room, half-naked with a towel around his torso, screaming because I had thrown out the tube of toothpaste, with at least two squeezes left (I thought him insane, but strangely, now relate to this idiocy).

However, he demands the best if going to the theater or to a concert or when taking a trip. We sit in the Founder's circle to see the touring Moiseyev dancers at the Los Angeles Music Center. And one December we stay at the Waldorf Astoria in New York prior to flying to Joh'burg to see Daddy's younger brother Henry. And certainly he spares no cost when purchasing tickets for High Holiday services.

One Saturday morning as I relax on the floor watching TV he informs, in all wisdom: "Cookie, I don't mean to be mean, but do you know how much you have cost me since you came to America? $10, 450.67."

I tell him he got off cheap, especially since he failed to ever send child support. But he does voice concerns regarding everyday living, and insists that I learn to drive carefully on the right, the "other side" of the road from the customary drive in South Africa, as well as in Britain and New Zealand. I take lessons from Sears on how to navigate those LA freeways; I can't possibly ask him for advice. My Dad "steers" a green Chevy coupe with silver wings and decorator panel. To put it mildly, he's a lunatic on the road; you could say a savage on wheels with scant use for signs while driving at unbelievable speeds, rarely putting down the brake. Yet he boasts of never having incurred an accident.

"Cookela," he cautions, "in Los Angeles you have to have four eyes. You never know where people are coming from." Yet he swerves in and out of traffic, cursing everything in sight. Naturally, in Yiddish.

It's the night of the Academy Awards in LA when my father pulls the Chevy out of the driveway and negotiates the Hollywood Freeway to take me to the hillside home of Aube Tzerko, the famed pedagogue with the shock of white/gray hair who has agreed to take me on as a student.

"Hee hee, I suppose you were watching the Oscars," my father tries small talk. Nope. Tzerko tests my ear training, hears me play and concludes that I may not have a major career in America, but could "enjoy a secondary one." He might even help me land a scholarship to UCLA where he's on staff.

I write the good news to my mother, adding that once and for all I'll knuckle under and learn all about theory, harmony and all that's required to become a better musician.

Meanwhile, my father rents me a small practice room at a busy music school on Fairfax, despite his disappointment that after all these years of study I fail to essay Liszt's Hungarian Rhapsody No. 2. "What kind of a pianist are you?"

But it gets harder and harder to concentrate, particularly the Friday morning when loudspeakers blare that a motorcade with Robert and Ethel Kennedy will be arriving at 10. Screw practicing! I slam the lid of the brown upright, pack up my scores and run to wait outside the drugstore at the corner of Fairfax and Santa Monica Boulevards for the entourage. This is why I'm here, in America, for the spirit of politics and camaraderie that I so sorely missed in Africa. I can hardly stand still, but nothing has prepared me for the sight of this exquisite, bronzed God who pulls up in an open limousine to stop at the light. I'm left speechless at the sight of Bobby Kennedy and amazed at his light hair. Ethel seems a bit too demure.

A letter arrives from my mother. She's offended at my wanting any scholarship, even one potentially from UCLA. "It's time you stopped being so selfish and considered your family for a change." I stare at her note. I don't get it, but looking at her scribbling, decide I can't fight any longer. It's time to give in and give up. (Now I wonder what might have been had she written, Go for it Greta. I may well have gone for it. May well have remained a pianist. May well have done, well, well.)

But I continue my studies, listlessly, and barely functioning. Tzerko, working two pianos side-by-side, demonstrates whatever sounds and/or interpretation he desires. Lessons can carry on for hours, and often I'm invited to sit in on the next student. I'm unused to such largesse. Afterwards, Tzerko drives me home on the way to his tennis game, chatting proudly of his association with pianist Misha Dichter. Sadly, I believe I've arrived at Tzerko's excellence too late. At one session I struggle with the fingering of Chopin's Revolutionary Étude. Fed up, Tzerko leaves me sitting at the bench for hours, while he eats lunch, shaves, and does whatever the hell he feels like doing. Still I fail to procure the desired phrasing. After six hours, he dismisses me. No matter the browbeating, nothing helps—too much has gone awry. I ask my father to call and say I won't be returning. Although it was hardly Tzerko's fault that I feel barely alive, he apparently sounded disappointed.

About 15 years later Tzerko notices my byline in the Los Angeles Times. He calls about one of his students, but makes no time to meet. If only I'd studied with him earlier, I may have had a chance at a career. Instead, I choose to close the piano, and literally not raise the lid for another 20 years.

Escape & Lenny

There was once a movie about actor Frances Farmer, starring Jessica Lange, who returns home to an abusive mother after having escaped to a better life. Fool, she thinks things will be different, because she's different. But she's wrong and ultimately succumbs to a mother-induced lobotomy.

After one year away, I too feel slightly homesick and honestly believe things will be better. In a way, it's good I left LA when I did because my father became extremely ill. He had to have his gallbladder removed, barely surviving a case of yellow jaundice. And as I've discovered, Daddy gets mean when he feels ill.

As the plane touches down at Jan Smuts Airport in Johannesburg, my mom and Auntie Gertie rush to greet me. Noticing my many rings on both hands, my mother shakes her head and whispers, conspiratorially: "Take them off, they don't look good, they look cheap." We drive back to Glen Isle flats, where a giant "Welcome Home Greta" banner floats out front. Relatives and friends toast me with cups of tea.

My mom has spared no expense for my homecoming. She's decorated my brother's old room at the back with a white lamp, dresser, bed, and lets me put up flags from all my travels to New York and London and San Francisco. "Everyone deserves their own room," she says, as though agreeing to some truth.

She also coordinates outings with boys I had previously dated & hated. Shrimpy Colin calls. While brushing her hair and fussing with her fringe in the mirror, my mother comments: "I hear you turned Colin down?" Then, seemingly shocked: "Just who do you think you are?"

I notice something different about my mom. She appears calmer, even happier since I left. She visits hairdressers regularly, and buys herself Italian knit sweaters—stuff I wish she'd done before rather than foisting her fashion sense on me. Of course, the converse turns out to be true. The more she's around me, the more disconcerting things become.

The biggest adjustment for my mother remains accepting my retirement from the concert stage. From going near any piano, actually. Rumors begin among the cognoscenti and a scandal soon mushrooms in the music world. Is Greta still playing? I hear it's all over?

One evening at an orchestral concert at City Hall, I'm crowded at intermission by acquaintances from the old days. Snoops demanding answers. I merely nod, attempting to deflect any growing tension. Suddenly, the mediocre and bespectacled local teacher, Mrs. Chertkow, grabs my wrists and holds my palms up to her immediate circle. "See, see she has long nails now; she's not playing, she's given up." I run, blindly, through the hall and into the garage, my loyal friend Marion following at the heel. We quickly slam the car doors and exit the parking lot.

Assuming a practical stance, my mother offers to pay for a controversial shorthand and typing course presented by two women she's met at the technical college. They guarantee results in six weeks; other methods span at least six months. I stay extra hours every day honing skills that later prove invaluable to me as a journalist. But long before the course completion, my mother demands I look for work. She's convinced I could head a movie studio or a large theatrical agency.

Instead, I secure a typing gig at Corlett Drive Estates, a realty firm headed by my brother's buddy Mike. "Of course, you're depressed," my brother acknowledges. "You're an intelligent girl, a pianist and you've been in America."

Meanwhile, my close friend Julie, a radiographer at the General Hospital, has moved to a hotel in busy Hillbrow. She encourages me to get a room there (I fancy that all meals are included in the rent). My brother concurs that it's time for me to get out of my mother's flat.

Sunday night I begin packing up my things. On a stepping stool, I retrieve from the hallway cupboard some of my wedding presents that have been stored on the top shelf. Mommy's chatting on the phone to Auntie Fanny. Taking time to prepare a sardine sandwich at the kitchen table, I become aware of my mother in the doorway. For years, I've debated the look burning her face that night. Hate will do.

"Hello Mommy," I smile. She raises her hand. I feel a sharp pain. What's that sound? I swear I can hear a young fawn crying in the distance, whimpering in its hurt. I look down. The kitchen floor is flooded with a pink liquid. I discover then that milk and blood mixed is quite beautiful. The next thing, I'm trapped in the bedroom. My left foot's bleeding badly. It's been sliced, near the bone of my big toe. Now well into her mad *Lucia di Lammermoor* act, my mother huffs and puffs, prancing in her bra and large pale pink panties, fielding me, preventing my escape.

I somehow make it out the door, race across the maroon-carpeted dining area, into the street, where I flag a motorist. I'll be damned if seconds before I close the back door, she doesn't slide in and say in her sweet soprano, "Please, please hurry, I must get my daughter to the hospital." In the emergency room, as the doctors attempt to pry out pieces of glass from that cursed milk bottle before stitching the wound, she leans over, and with eyes large and eyebrows raised warns, *schweig* (shut up).

My brother arrives to drive us home. I feel some kind of internal relief; at last, I'll get some sympathy. Strange, he's assuming his I'll-forgive-you-even-if-you've-done-wrong attitude. Then my beloved Auntie Fanny comes into my room, as I lay back in bed exhausted. "Don't be so selfish next time," she says. I can only wonder at what my mother told her followers.

No apology. On the contrary, it's business as usual Monday. She insists I go to work at the real estate company. "Go on, you're not so fragile," she reiterates her customary response whenever there looms any specter of her impropriety. I incur six stitches, and drag my left leg. Ten days later I return to hospital. They reopen the wound to get out more glass. In serious situations we always take taxis, but this day my mother opts for the bus. Struggling the two blocks up the hill, I venture, almost inaudibly.

"You hurt me; how could you?"
"Well, you...Never mind, Dondela, let's not talk about it again." We never did. And I never tell anyone about the attack.

Above all, my mother's fed up about her carpet. She takes great pride in her stupid edge-to-edge carpeting in the living and dining rooms. Now the carpet's colored even darker, flooded with my wet red blood, and has to be lifted up and sent to the cleaners. Takes days to get back.

There are other immeasurable repercussions. I stop menstruating for ten months. My mother decides I must be pregnant—I'm dating Eddie with the curly hair at the time—and she demands an invasive internal exam with the family physician Joe. Eventually, I consult a gynecologist, a gentle soul with piercing blue eyes, who grows angry at any implication of pregnancy. He prescribes a fertility drug and all returns to normal within three days.

I'd better return fast to America. How could I have let my green card go? I visit the U.S. Consulate downtown, and to my relief, initiate a new immigration process. I pray, once more, as I write to Daddy, asking for a return ticket. He quickly agrees.

In the interim, I meet Lenny, a short, stocky, cocky and almost-prizefighter attorney who maintains in the face of all difficulties, "I'm always right, doll; I'm always right." Happy-go-lucky, Lenny takes me to his friends to play pool or card games. One night we sit around the living room floor dealing Monopoly. Joy, oh sweet joy, I'm actually winning, with lots of money and property stashed in my corner. I'm ready to rock, and build three hotels. With a lusty laugh, Lenny announces that there are NO little red hotels left in the box.

"Sorry you lost, doll," he smirks.
"Well, put something in place of those little red houses; find a substitute symbol."
"Oh no," his grin grows as he takes a hefty puff on a cigarette. "There can be no substitutes; it's in the rules."
Ultimately I lose the game. I still hate Lenny for it.

But Lenny loves life, and when we get beneath the sheets, he enjoys himself. He drives me home around 4 a.m.

Ever-anxious to thwart my defection to America, my mother urges marriage. The first clue of dissent comes when a lethargic Lenny opts to wait in the car, while sending me upstairs to a jeweler friend of his to pick up a whopper of a diamond ring he has ordered. No need to also see it, doll. Trouble quickly brews at the engagement party that Saturday night. There I am in a see-through black lace mini when Lenny confronts.

"Tell your mother to take back the money; I'll choose my own flat."
Huh?
Without my knowledge, let alone consent, my mother apparently had paid off a landlord in an upscale old *Yente* building that she'd always hungered after. I convey Lenny's extreme displeasure.
"Hmmm, hmmmm, o--kay," she responds, in a sweet singsong.

But once the guests depart she's far from docile about yet another imagined loss. There I am, literally on the toilet, when she barges in. "You little bitch you; you're only getting a small fridge. Everybody has a ****-size fridge. You rotter you."

A silver soup spoon descends down hard on my right hand. I don't know what she's talking about, but oh, my knuckle hurts. I've never discussed a lousy fridge, let alone its dimensions with Lenny. He'd surely opt for lesser is better anyway. I have little use for such household trivia.

Out of nowhere and from way inside a voice instructs quietly: "Greta, your second marriage will go the same way as the first with Ralph. It was not your fault. But if you stay in South Africa, you will be killed." I know then that soon I'll be gone. I'm calm; no need to think about it further.

Weeks pass, and at the scheduled wedding rehearsal, Lenny shows up at synagogue a half-hour late, dressed in raggedy blue shorts and chewing gum. I seize my chance. "Watch, he'll stand us BOTH up at the altar," I tell my mother who turns white. I phone the reluctant groom-to-be.

"You don't want to get married do you?"
"I honestly don't doll," he replies, sweetly. "I hope you don't mind." (Out of fear of her, I return the ring. I could kick myself; can you imagine what that huge rock would go for?)

On Wednesday, I call my Dad. I'm terrified he's changed his mind.
"Of course, I'll send you a ticket. You know I will. But I don't understand why you got engaged in the first place."

Time to pack. Oh, oh, there's Mommy. Glaring. But I grab that small window of opportunity with both hands, and on Saturday depart for America via Europe, leaving behind, forever, friends Phyllie and Julie, Auntie Gertie, Uncle Louis, Belle, Sol, Bessie, Tooksie. Also my beloved Morris mini-minor, and my important rock vinyls, namely Elvis and Cliff Richard. And, you could say God—if there exists one in that place, in that time, in that country.

Arriving in London on what was supposed to be my wedding day, I dance through the streets of Kensington, parodying from "My Fair Lady":

> *"Ohhh, I'm **not** getting married in the morning; ding dong the bells are **not** gonna chime...."*

On Nov. 1, 1970, with one suitcase, I arrive at Los Angeles International Airport. Once more, my bandy-legged Daddy waits to greet me. Without fuss, we travel directly to his apartment in West Hollywood. To pick up where we left off.

BROTHERLY BETRAYAL

My brother's on the phone calling from South Africa. *"Howwwwwwzit?* I'm coming to the States; I'm coming to see you."

I haven't seen him in nearly six months. Not since I migrated to California and reunited with Daddy. We're sharing a furnished apartment mere blocks from, gasp, Hollywood Boulevard.

Three years my senior, my brother plans to visit Las Vegas and suggests we meet up at Caesars Palace. I register late morning at the hotel and check into a large pink chamber dubbed Cleopatra's room; my brother later unpacks next door. Oh, how great to see him again. How's his marriage going? And what's it like working with über-pushy father-in-law? Oh, how I miss the lunches we so enjoyed at the plush Carlton Hotel in downtown Johannesburg near his accounting office. Remember how good the salmon salads used to be?

But we've all moved on *n'est-ce pas?* Big shots, we're now on the Vegas Strip. My brother lounges on the bed watching TV; I'm mesmerized on the edge. Suddenly he lunges.

"What the hell is wrong with you?" I half-giggle, half-frown, half-protest.
"You don't love me," he mumbles. Pulls open my sash. Boy is he weird. And boy is he grumpy.
The next day we fly to LA.

"Heee heee heee," my father celebrates the 5'11," brown-eyed boy presenting at his front door. Smiles all around. Soon talk centers on the usual (whites only) South Africanisms, about how much money my brother and so and so are making, and who's bought a new mansion, and whose husband is messing with whom.

And yes, of course, he'd love to meet Greta's new pals, Maggie, Margie and Pat. With Daddy all stretched out at home watching TV, my brother treats the gang to dinner and many drinks at a dark, plant-filled Polynesian palace. Paying the bill with bravado, he exits with married Maggie.

"Why would he come to visit us and then stay out all night?" my father asks, face flushed. Envy, perhaps? He's happy though to have his son shell out for brunch the next day at Canter's, the 24-hour deli around the corner in the Jewish quarter. Favoring a meal of matzo ball soup and rye, my brother boasts of his many "conquests" back home. Seems all the Jewish wives in Africa are after him.

Who cares, I'm just happy to have a father for the first time in my life. I did tell you that he sailed for America when I was 10 without saying goodbye, right? Now he's 62.

"Hee hee hee, my Cookela, we two are doing well, aren't we?" my Dad beams Saturday mornings, as I sit under the turquoise hooded hairdryer he purchased especially from Sears. "Cookela, you look so beautiful," he marvels Saturday nights, as I ready for dates. However, he's concerned about the late nights. "Never stay over at a man's house; he'll never respect you." I don't laugh; nor do I ever spend nights away.

"Cookela, Coookie, come quick, Johannesburg's on the line." This time, my brother's anticipating a three-week visit, partly for business and to take a break, we surmise, from the pressures associated with new fatherhood.

My brother calls to say he's at the Beverly Hilton Hotel. I steer my old blue Plymouth into the parking lot, then ride the elevator to his green-and-white suite. I reach to kiss his cheek. He holds on long. Very long.

"You know what's wrong with you...." I stay in his grip. He breathes heavily, leans back; rubs against me, up and down, side to side. I vomit silently, without sound, or bile.

"I want to *jol*," he says. We go shopping. First, a shoe store on Rodeo Drive. A beautiful young woman kneels at his feet, slipping on an $80 pair of Italian shoes. "Keep it up honey; I like my women this way." He buys me a Gucci watch, paying $200 for a round red-and-navy dial with matching navy strap. He hugs my waist. "I bought you this because I love you; not because I like you."

I return home to West Hollywood to change clothes then return to his hotel. He decides a bath is in order before we head out to dinner. And demands I keep him company.

"No, I won't."
"You're so cold and pathetic." Sitting alongside the tub, I remove my glasses. Never thought I'd be so grateful to be shortsighted (Americans call it myopic). My brother splashes about, this way and that, as if the scenario represents the norm.

I tell the very tall, gray-haired psychotherapist I've been seeing in Beverly Hills-adjacent that I want those damn baths to stop. This professor, head of a training program at a major California university, merely blows me a kiss. "The day you stand up to him, I'll be so proud of you."
How do I do that?"
"You just do it," says this so-called expert in family relations.

But these are early days in the self-help field, the mid-1970s, and even the counselor can't comprehend how to combat this immovable force, this brick wall I must confront.

What's happening here? Why can't my brother behave normally and take me out for dinners and movies and things like before? Why can't we just be ordinary?

Summertime in Europe, and my brother says to please join him in London and, thrill upon thrills, he promises we'll fly to the Channel Isles, a place of mystery forever fascinating to me. He'll be ok this time. Surely.

We register at London's fancy The Selfridge, a hotel near Oxford Street. (Closed in 2008, this establishment is dubbed, "The Old Selfridges.") My brother demands we share quarters.
"I want my own room."
"Listen my girl; money doesn't grow on trees. You have to learn to economize or you'll have nothing." (Shall I demand the hotel clerk give me my own space? What if she says no? What shall I do?)

We browse at the dress shop downstairs. He selects a skirt and matching top in shimmering, almost kaleidoscopic colors. "Walk this way," he breathes outside the dressing room. "Walk to the door; turn this way, turn that."

We retire. I crawl into the bed with a white duvet. A white night stand with a radio stands guard between us. I'm asleep. Suddenly He's on top of me. "Why are you so mean to me?" There's some talk about giving me $500. I laugh as my chest tightens.
"Please get off."
"You're so cold."

I enter the white-tiled bathroom and hear my retching. My insides are now brave enough to openly rebel. When I return, he's facing the wall. "You're not nice to me," he mumbles on and on—and whenever he sees me in the years to come. In fact, should you meet he'll probably tell you the same thing.

In the morning, we fly the short distance to the isles. My brother plans to float a company in that tax haven and is off to the lawyers. I stand at the shore fronting the lovely hotel, skimming stones, beating the chill. I go in for a bath then warm my soul with a large, fluffy white towel, kept nice and toasty on a gold electric wall rack. I swear if ever I make it rich, I'll install a towel heater in my bathroom.

At dinner my brother's brown eyes are frozen. While chewing a filet mignon cooked well, he sneers out of nowhere: "Listen, don't you ever look in the mirror and think, 'how can I make myself more sensuous for a man?'" I'm in my late 20s, weigh all of 98 pounds and know well how my body appears to men.

"How can you say this to me?" I start crying.
"Listen, my girl are you starting your nonsense again?"

To him it's all nonsense.

SOMETHING ABOUT INCEST

There was once a television drama called, "Something about Amelia," with Ted Danson and Glenn Close. The story is about a young girl and a father who won't leave her alone. He keeps pestering her. He stands on the landing, leering. All she wants to do is go to bed. This is how my brother looks at me—with that same disrespectful leer. No matter what this poor teenager in the film does, no matter how she begs, he won't stop. My brother too ignores me. No matter what I say, or do, it doesn't make any difference. It must take a special skill to be taken seriously, to have people listen and respect when you say no. Obviously I'm no good at it.

STRANGE HAPPENINGS
IN SANTA MONICA

I live in Santa Monica, California, about 19 blocks from the beach, and enjoy a boyfriend, a nice newly-graduated Jewish doctor. Six-foot plus, muscular and bearded, I first hail Dr. K at a New Year's Eve party at a friend's house in Bel-Air. He looks amazing in blue denims and a matching shirt, and we talk until 4 a.m. We soon develop our Saturday night routine: Disco dancing at Dillon's in Westwood near UCLA. We like moving to Thelma Houston's "Don't Treat Me This Way." On the dance floor I fantasize that I'm a famous writer and visualize my byline all over the place.

I've been with Dr. K on a couple of trips, first to Honolulu, and then last summer to Tahiti. We stopped off at Bora Bora, flying into the most beautiful airstrip imaginable, where the plane comes to rest at the brink of exquisitely turquoise waters. Later, we disembarked at Club Med

Moorea. Luckily, he brought his black bag along, because our camp was plagued with dengue fever, and there also resulted assorted infections from insect bites and coral cuts. Things got so hectic I told the approaching sick that the good doctor, a veterinarian, could be of no help.

A medical intern, Dr. K lives alone in a crappy West LA apartment. He's always half dead from exhaustion. And moi? With my father resettled in South Africa, I've moved into a rent-controlled, two-bedroom apartment with friend Marsha, a blonde bombshell with a cat and a Cadillac whom I met shortly after my arrival in California.

At first, I'm shy about sex with Dr. K, but I must say I've been feeling more and more brazen lately. I'm even considering opening the door naked. Whenever Marsha takes off for a weekend, we occupy her giant king size bed with its faux leopard-skin bedspread and floral headboard.

Last Saturday night we had such a good laugh. Oohing and aahing as I rubbed my thighs so deliciously together, I suddenly became aware of two golden eyes fixated on me. Seems Marsha's little cat, January, had crawled into the nightstand drawer. She peered at us in wonder.

After bopping around as a freelance this-and-that writer, I've recently been brought on board as an entertainment reporter/assistant editor for the Santa Monica Evening Outlook. I started out doing classical music reviews, and graduated to covering pop, theater and even opera. However, I feel too identified with the artistic process to continue writing criticism. Rather, I opt for features and news stories regarding many incredible artists. At the Santa Monica regional daily I profile personalities such as soprano Beverly Sills, TV's Connie Chung, also Pete Seeger, Van Cliburn, the Village People and Ben Weisman who wrote many of Elvis's hits, to name a few. More big name interviews in the movie and fine arts world will come later.

But these days we're really pressured at the paper, especially putting out the Friday tab. Of all things my brother just phoned to say he's coming to town next weekend. I'm upset. He met Marsha awhile back, and to my deep chagrin took her out, slept with her apparently or so he boasted, and now he wants to stay with us and no doubt date her again. He's also demanding a party.

"I don't want you staying with us," I repeat.
"Lizzen my girl, I'm coming."
I plead with Marsha. "Listen Gretie, what can I do; he says he's coming."

My week turns increasingly lousy:
* Tuesday: It's one of our lighter days, and Editor Judy takes me for a salad lunch at fast foodie Pete's in Santa Monica. I don't feel that great.
* Tuesday night: I have dinner with a friend at the top of a fancy hotel on Fourth Street in Santa Monica. We have drinks, and I stare fascinated as a young waitress loads six orders way up high on her tray. She trips on a ruffle in the carpet, and in slow motion, I watch the guacamole and cream and Mexican rice and salsa and lettuce and

refried beans begin their descent towards my lap. Soon, I'm covered in enchiladas. Screaming for ice, I rush to the restroom, cursing everything in sight. The maître d' hands me a chit promising to take care of the dry-cleaning bill for my ruined skirt. The way things turn out I don't get to claim my satisfaction.

* Wednesday morning: I don't feel good.

* Wednesday night: At an outdoor concert of Captain & Tennille at the Greek Theater, I discover a tender lump in my groin, but not before having to contend with Marsha's stupid maroon Cadillac breaking down half-way up the hill and causing traffic to snake for easily an hour. My doctor says I must come in for blood tests.

* Friday: I faint as they take blood at his mid-Wilshire office. "This is not like you Greta," the good doctor says, adding that his colleague will be on call that weekend. Tests reveal a high white cell count, indicative of an infection.

* Friday night: My fever is 102. I'm delirious. I call the colleague on-call. Then Marsha calls him. Take aspirin and rest, he says, refusing to see me.

Saturday my brother arrives, chest puffed, huffing in and out of Marsha's apartment. Fever's climbing, I'm shaking uncontrollably. Brother demands that Marsha accompany him to a movie in Santa Monica.

"I'm worried about Gretie,"

"She'll be fine," he insists.

They go to a movie on 14th Street, five blocks away. Marsha calls from the cinema. No answer. She panics, and over my brother's protestations, rushes home. She finds me lying on the bathroom tile under an open window, gasping for air. She tries calling Dr. K, but a recording informs that his telephone is no longer in working order; turns out he hasn't paid the bill. Marsha hops into her Caddy and goes to his West Los Angeles apartment. He comes rushing over. He calls my doctor's partner and in the most threatening tone warns that should I not immediately be admitted to Cedars-Sinai hospital that he, Dr. K, will make sure the practitioner never works again. We await the ambulance.

As I lie back on the tile, my brother enters the bathroom. He picks up a wash cloth and runs it under the cold faucet. "You're so hot, I'll get you ready," he says. He lifts up my nightgown and proceeds to wash my breasts, up and down, with the cloth. My eyes promise me they'll never forget.

The doctor meets us in the lobby. I'm like a rag doll that keeps collapsing. My liver count is way up high, and the physician who has refused to see me apologizes for his previous lack of concern. I'm rushed into a room and finally relax as an intravenous drip is inserted. Over the next few hours and days people come in and out to take blood and attend to me wearing assorted space costumes because they have no idea what disease I have. And this was way before AIDS. Finally, blood cultures determine mononucleosis, apparently uncommon at age 32. Complications set in. I get pleurisy, then hepatitis. My brother and Marsha have painful shots in their bums to immunize them.

My brother stops by the hospital often. One night he gifts me a copy of the bestseller, "Roots." He doesn't hand me the book, but rather places it on a shelf and kicks it towards the bed. "Listen my girl I have three kids to consider," he explains seeing my look. Playing God, he declines to alert my parents about my illness, insisting that when he returns to South Africa he'll allow them to contact me, probably from his office phone so it won't cost too much.

Dr. K meanwhile annoys me. He never comes to see me during visiting hours, but arrives way after 10 p.m. Unbeknownst to me, he stays all night to make sure I'm ok, and offers to be of help. But I fail to notice his abiding goodness.

The treating physicians express concern. My temperature keeps climbing. My nightly deliriums continue. Now I imagine the pictures on the walls are moving. A kindly nurse saves me, suggesting that around midnight when the fever is at its worst and even the fever reducers haven't helped that I request a bucket of chopped ice. It works. I suck until dawn and the shaking subsides, but my robes are changed sometimes seven times a night because of sweats. I devise an effective visualization. I see myself at the head of a giant staircase in a garden of what many years later on a visit to France I recognize as the grounds at the palace at Versailles. But now, the greenery and serenity and terraces and roses are all in my mind, providing peace and snatches of sleep.

There transpires a world event of monumental importance during my hospital stay. On August 16, 1977, a somber and nervous Marsha and David deliver the bad news: Elvis Presley has passed away. I can't live without Elvis, or his music. He kept my teenager sane. Both my brother and I had attained a measure of serenity, even great joy many a night in our red-carpeted lounge, taking turns to rock to yet another Elvis hit spinning on the turntable. My mother usually left us alone at such moments.

Losing Elvis is just the worst; things at the hospital are hardly better. X-rays reveal that fluid is increasing in my lungs and my physician wants to give it three more days and then start draining. Also, there's talk about problems surrounding my heart. I have no concept of how ill I am; I just want to recover quickly so I can go back to reporting. Overworked Entertainment Editor Judith Bloom has come by a few times. In her generosity, she's still keeping my job open at the paper. I tell a story that the other morning an African-American male nurse, dressed in white well-pressed pants and starched shirt, stood over my bed and told me to get well because there were stories that needed to be done. Everyone insists it was but a dream. I think otherwise.

Friday morning: my brother appears contrite. He has to leave and go to Seattle on business. He still insists, "iz not necessary" to notify my parents.

* Friday afternoon: Brother leaves. His plane departs at 2:30.
* Saturday morning: My doctor comes by and takes my temperature. "What's going on here?" he asks. My fever has dropped to 99.

* Saturday afternoon: Barely a sign of pleurisy, fluid has receded. Heart's looking good.
* Sunday afternoon: Back home with Marsha in Santa Monica. Feel very fragile. She brings me food. I drop the glass of water and start sobbing. She agrees to forgive this, and then asks what about the rent money? I feebly write a check, but feel like a pathetic Joan Crawford at the mercy of Bette Davis in the horror schlock, "What Ever Happened to Baby Jane." I expect a rat to materialize at any moment on my dinner plate.

A week later my mother calls. She's shocked. In her best British voice, she asks to speak to Marsha. "Thank you for looking after Greta," she says. Then a pause. "A mother thanks you." My Dad calls from my brother's office, and offers to come over and live with me again. No thanks.

I feel stronger, and two weeks later am chatting with Dr. K in his old beat-up green car in the parking lot of Dillon's disco.

"Your poor brother was nearly out of his mind with worry about his 'kid sister'," Dr. K informs.
"My brother has been molesting me for six years," I say quietly.
"Oh God." Dr. K, bless him, pounds his fists through the junky dashboard. "I could kill that sonofabitch."

A few months later I agree to meet my brother who's scouting Toronto for a possible move with his family. They're planning to immigrate to Canada, and he's checking out an ice cream parlor on the waterfront for possible purchase.

We stroll along the promenade. Leaning on the railing overlooking dark waters, I quietly tell him that I've told Dr. K about the molestation.

"Oh, so you told him," he says evenly, and with only the slightest blanch. Then without missing a beat: "Please don't tell my wife. It will break up my marriage."

I never do.

Fast Forward ten years: Sneers and jeers continue. My brother's taken to phoning me around 1 a.m., California time. When I protest, he laughs. But of considerable concern are his calls to the newsroom of the Los Angeles Times. After years of freelancing as a music writer and sometimes arts editor, I've been named Calendar Editor of the Orange County edition of the Times. Yes, it's pretty prestigious and intense. Recognizing my knowledge of the arts and also my immersion in pop culture, the Times has entrusted me to build up coverage of the local arts scene.

Thursdays of course, rank the busiest at the paper as we put finishing touches to Friday's all-important Calendar section what with local listings and film reviews and pop and classical music coverage. This afternoon, I've just emerged from a major meeting and feel pretty good about the section. Publisher Tom Johnson has praised my work and invited me to a luncheon next week with the Big Shots downtown in the Picasso Room. I hear my name paged. "Your brother's calling," the switchboard operator announces to the entire newsroom. Must be an emergency.

"Howzit," my brother begins the typical African greet. I describe how well things are going and that our coverage is bringing in more readers and bigger audiences to concerts, even art exhibitions and how I enjoy going up to LA for meetings and also having fun with the Orange County editors going to all those weird business functions we attend in the name of community goodwill.

"That's nice….. (Pause) But do you have man?" I hear his breathing.
"How dare you ask me such rubbish?" He laughs. I literally feel the previous pride start its familiar draining. It takes weeks to recover from this episode.
No, I'm lying. It's been decades and the disbelief rages still.

Fast forward to Johannesburg, 1992. I'm back in Johannesburg after my mom's passing. My brother, whom I have talked to minimally during the last eight years, invites himself to tea at the posh Sandton Sun hotel. He won't stay long.

I stand atop the giant staircase off the lobby, curious to see how he looks. He appears heavier, with a thick head of gray hair. We enter the plush dining room. "Jesus Christ," he says, spying the price tag for afternoon tea. I smile, knowing that with the exchange rate I can divide the cost by 3 and readily afford the $8 for a lavish spread of sandwiches of salmon and cucumber, cake, strawberries and cream, and hot scones, all accompanied by pots of Earl Grey tea.

As we chat, mostly about my mother's impossible life, my brother declares: "Now that this foolishness between us is over, I want you to tell my kids everything is ok with us. Do you understand?"

Without wasting a second: "Would you like me to tell them about the incest?"
"No, please don't; it will ruin my relationship with them."

He chats away about his friends and his encounters with various relatives before concluding: "I'm a good person, Greta. I've never knowingly harmed anyone."

Funny, in the skies en route to Johannesburg I had told myself something similar. That he hadn't really meant anything by it all; really it hadn't been so bad. Some call this minimizing; others deem it being in denial. I've always just longed for ordinary with my brother, to be able to discuss movies we both like, concerts, plays, his friends, my friends, his dreams, my journeys, the stock market, my job....

Quietly—if I'm aggressive he gets louder—I venture to tell my brother that he has caused me tremendous damage. Because of you, I say, I don't trust men fully. "I understand fully what you are saying," my brother responds, "but lizzen, I once looked inside when I was in Toronto and I got very depressed. I'm not prepared to do it again."

I don't tell him what it's like being stimulated by triggers in the world: For example, how creepy I felt when the camera zoomed in on Robert Redford's neck in the film, "Havana." Or how my doctor's wavy salt-and-pepper hairline evokes eerie sensations whenever we consult. I remind myself, these are but remembrances, ghosts of things past.

"You and I will never discuss that subject again do you understand," my brother tries, as we re-enter the hotel lobby. He wishes me well, and pleads for us to stay in touch.

"You know I'll never hurt you again. I was very insecure back then." With a cocked, slightly crazed grin, he delivers his coup de grace: "Besides, you won't let me. You're much too aware now."

DADDY I MISS YOU

Before landing my big gig as numero uno arts editor in Orange County, I flourish while renting a furnished studio at Oakwood Gardens, an apartment complex in Toluca Lake with two pools and Jacuzzis frequented by many in the movie and television industry who've come to LA to be near Disney or Warner Studios down the hill. I make friends with Fiona and Alex, my neighbors downstairs, and often borrow their marmalade cat for a few hours and until Fiona fetches him after a late-night date. Many times we scour the bushes for Morris, praying the coyotes haven't gotten to him first.

Writing a lot, I profile for the Times pianist Radu Lupu— before his Rasputin look. The gloriously sensitive, chain-smoking pianist scheduled to perform all five Beethoven Concertos at the Hollywood Bowl, confides he gets so nervous prior to a performance that he throws up backstage. A couple of months later I meet Lupu's close friend, another gloriously sensitive soul, pianist Murray Perahia whom I interview at his suite at a mid-town Sheraton.

Perahia recalls having had a normal childhood spent with loving parents and no pressure. I could have done without that bit of information. In fact, following most interviews with classical musicians, I come home and cry.

Yesterday I was at the Times in downtown LA when my brother called to invite me to Toronto for his son's bar mitzvah. The only way my brother believes he can get my mother to make the journey is to hatch a mass family exodus from Johannesburg. So he's paid the fares of cousins Belle and her brother Barney, anticipating correctly that my mother would be shamed into coming to Canada.

I have not seen her in nearly a decade. Now, in the spacious living room of my brother's suburban home my elder cousin—you know, the one with the gummy hip, that self-proclaimed righteous great cook and family saint—emerges and attempts to block my path. "Mom is over there," she points to my mother, blonde and bejeweled, seated in an armchair. At 32, I'm reed-thin, wearing a tight black skirt and red shirt, black stockings and matching pumps. My hair, highlighted, looks sleek and natural.

"Hello Mommy."
My mother cocks her head. "And who are you? I'm afraid I don't know you."

"I'm your daughter." (There's nothing weird here I keep telling myself.)

Later, while I'm sipping tea, she comes over. "They all say I shouldn't have said that to you. I apologize. But how do you think 'a' mother feels seeing her daughter look so old?"

But my Dad impresses all. The tainted one, he exhibits a quiet dignity, emerging gentle and polite and charming in his new blue suit. He expresses sadness that my brother paid for all the relatives to come over from Africa, yet he must pay his own way. I imagine my brother deems the retribution just.

The band's playing and my father asks me to dance. Oh, what a joy to waltz with Daddy after all these years, to step 1, 2, 3, 1, 2, 3, holding him close. As we traverse the floor, I swear I see an apparition. There's my mother, the pleats of her absurdly girlish light-blue dress swishing this way and that, bobbing between us, trying to end our partnership. I refuse all eye contact, and she's left to shake her curls in mad disapproval.

As midnight strikes, she literally emits a caterwauling moan, and is rushed to a Toronto hospital, complaining of severe stomach pains. She undergoes tests, which my brother naturally pays for. Turns out, my mother has cramps and just needs a good pooh.

"How are you Mommy," I enter her ward.

"Go on, man. Here; take my panties." She throws her soiled undergarments my way.

(That voice. That contempt. Becomes an echo almost a decade later during a screening of the sensuous movie, "Like Water for Chocolate." Here, in one famous scene, the tortured daughter must bathe her awful mother who snarls at her slowness. "Give it to me," she demands a towel. At least this girl pulls faces behind her mother's back and plots revenge. The audience collectively groans; I find the tone strangely familiar.)

A few months following the bar mitzvah, my father begins experiencing chest pains. He's diagnosed in Johannesburg with lung cancer and is expected to live no more than three months. But then Daddy smoked his entire life, starting as a young boy standing around and shivering in the snow. Daddy recounted often how cold life had been growing up in Eastern Europe, in the city of Riga and environs.

My brother volunteers a ticket for me to visit my ailing father in South Africa. We go together, and upon arrival immediately head for the residential hotel in Hillbrow where Daddy resides, on the same floor as his brother Henry. I'm suffering the effects of severe jet lag; flying from New York for nearly 17 hours proves a killer. I prefer to take my time going via London where, after a night's rest, one can board the plane around the same time zone as Johannesburg.

I curl up on a small sofa under an open window in my Dad's room and fall into the deepest slumber. My brother leaves on an errand. Half conscious, I hear the sound of distant thunder, observe a sliver of lighting and feel raindrops splashing on the sill, but remain too fatigued to pull the covers, let alone close the window. But excuse me; is there not a parent in the room?

"I should have closed that damn window, but ach, you know how I am when I'm sick," my father later excuses his oversight. Shivering and wet I awake two hours later, and know I'm in for it. I've caught that hideous flu doing the rounds and run a very high fever. But I keep on going another five days trying to conclude research on a Sunday piece I'm preparing for the Times regarding the local classical music scene. Segregation's slowly on the wane, and concert halls and theaters start opening up to all races. I interview the director of the Performing Arts Council Transvaal (PACT) in Pretoria, and tour the University of Witwatersrand campus and its music department.

By the weekend I'm bed-bound, and hardest of all, my ears hurt, feeling horribly clogged. I ask my brother to call a specialist. Two days pass. Bad Days. Still he hasn't called. Of course I should have contacted the doctor myself, but I've been well trained to turn my power off. And suffer. Later, I almost faint in the waiting room of the ear, nose and throat guy.

"I'm more worried about my father who has cancer than her ears," my brother informs the doctor. Surgery appears the best option, to have grommets inserted in both ears to drain the fluid, enabling me to later fly back to LA.

Finally discharged after days in the hospital, we walk down a tunnel to the car. "Do you have any idea how much you've cost me," my brother says, then admits his father-in-law has proffered a check to cover all costs.

At the hotel, we're enjoying breakfast in the dining room. My brother leaves to take an important call from overseas. "Who was that?"
"The rabbi from Toronto."
"What did he want?"
"He called because he heard my sister's so ill."
"I'm your sister."
"Listen my girl, this is serious. It's no joke."
Guess he doesn't see me there.

My brother stays close to my Dad. I'll never forget how he stares at my father from the base of the hospital bed, almost as though regarding the image of say Moses. Perhaps even Jesus. My brother forever comes to resent my mother's refusal to allow us any peace with our father or his memory.

"You have noooooo right coming here to see your father," she pronounced after our arrival in Johannesburg. "He deserves to die like a dog." Well, he didn't. His son, at his side until the end, got to know him, love him and ultimately bury him with dignity and appreciation.

My brother too helps orchestrate my goodbyes. Home in California, I quickly enter my usual trance, concentrating only on my newspaper-gal working ambition. After three weeks, my brother calls.

"Greta, for God's sake, why haven't you called? The man is dying. Don't you get it?" Rocketed out of my slumber, I immediately phone at midnight my time. Gasping for air, my Dad comes on the line. "Jankela," I cite my pet name for my father. "Jankela, everything is such shit. I'm working so hard."

I'm doing what I always do best with my Dad: Kvetch.
"I have to go," he gasps. And dies three hours later.

Dear Daddy,

I miss you. I wish I'd known you more. If only you were alive today, I'd take you to concerts and buy you dinner and would demand that you have friends in this world. I'm a journalist you know, and can pretty much get tickets to all the events. I know, you want to go and listen to those Three Tenors. I love Pavarotti too.

I'll take you up on your offer and go with you to synagogue on the High Holidays. I'd love to sit next to you and pray. I'm sorry I always refused to go, but I was so appalled that people have to pay in America to attend services. We could go to movies as we did when I first arrived. Remember the time you snuck us in to the back row to see 'The Graduate' when there were lines and lines of people. You fooled the usher saying you had to use the facilities. I thought you were a genius.

Daddy, I only knew you five years and it was not enough time, damn it. Sadly, I brought to that time Mommy's hatred and never really gave you a chance. For that, I'm so sorry and ask your forgiveness.

I wonder if you were ever proud of me. I'm so sorry I wasn't with you at the end, but I know how important it was that your son was

145

there. I do believe he learned to love you with all his heart, and he's so sad he didn't know you better. He also carried Mommy's bitterness.

I observed Yahrzeit at a Reform synagogue in Encino. You would have died if you'd heard the rabbi. I swear he sang the Kaddish, are you ready for this, accompanied on guitar to 'The Girl from Ipanema.' I almost plotzed thinking of your reaction.

I have sat on the patio at Oakwood Apartments, crying desperately for you. I was at first inconsolable and my friends Cynthia and Fiona didn't know how to approach me. Then after one week the mantle of grief that had descended on me just lifted—fast, suddenly, and unexpectedly. In one swoop I was back into the pull of my life.

Daddy, I've seen you in my dreams over the years. Sometimes, thrashing about late at night, I imagine I'm in bed in Johannesburg and think I hear you crying for me from America. (Of course, other times, I swear I can hear Mommy calling me from Africa and wake up not knowing if I'm asleep in Joh'burg or LA.)

But I know one sure thing. Music is what we shared. Passionately. So let us sing our favorite arias, and admire a piano piece or two. And I promise the next time I visit South Africa I will stop by your grave at the Westside Jewish Cemetery to celebrate your life and acknowledge my deep loss.

I love you Jankela. Always. Your daughter, Greta.

Orange County
Beware

Walking in the parking garage at the Oakwood apartments
late one night, I suddenly become aware of two heavyset
men approaching. Terrified, I keep on walking. So do they.
I imagine I'm in some TV plot and about to die. I go faster,
they come closer. I slow down, so do they. Pretty soon we
meet face to face. That's it; I'm a goner.

"Excuse me miss," the shorter one says. I await the deathblow.
"Would you care to subscribe to the L.A. Times?"
So relieved, I could kill the kid.
"Are you crazy; I work for them," is all I manage, before
heading off to building X and apartment No. 304.

The Hollywood Bowl season is underway at nearby Cahuenga Pass. I'm thrilled to interview pianist Ivo Pogorelich, who after much international press makes his West Coast debut in Prokofieff's Third Concerto. Contrary to his bad-boy poster image, he's charming.

Twice weekly I journey the 60 miles down to the Times's Orange County newsroom to help edit reviews and features. After 18 months of shuttling between bureaus, I'm hired as chief arts person. What a constant juggling act deciding which Los Angeles stories to yank, and which local OC creations to place in their stead. Much time is spent mollycoddling the downtown critics and editors and powers that be.

Still wanting the prestige of a byline in all editions, I continue on occasion to write for downtown Calendar. One Sunday piece, "The Aches and Pains of a Decade's Promising Pianists," that spills over two pages and chronicles the crippling injuries of pianists Leon Fleisher, Byron Janis and Gary Graffman, proves a prophetic foreshadowing of my own future disabilities.

Working long days on both Daily Calendar and a special glossy the Times puts out on the opening of the new Orange County Performing Arts Center I begin experiencing screaming pains in my neck, upper back and arms. The diagnosis? Repetitive stress injury. Typewriters have disappeared forever from newsrooms, and I've been slogging away on a new computer with a stiff keyboard placed any which way on my desk. Ergonomics is not yet in the vernacular—let alone the diagnosis of carpal tunnel syndrome or fibromyalgia—and I'm one of the first of more than 200 staffers at the paper to experience painful symptoms and injury.

To its credit, the Times eventually acknowledges the problem, retrofitting the newsroom—one of the first media outfits to do so—with adjustable desks and wrist rests and headphones and things at considerable cost. But for me the damage is done.

SKITTELS

Sunday morning. I've just returned from a coffee and bagel brunch at the apartment clubhouse when I receive a call from Africa. Bad news: My much-loved cousin Hedy-Anne, whom I nicknamed Skittels since childhood, has ended her life back in Joh'burg. Apparently, just before her 40th birthday, she gave the maid the weekend off, closed the curtains to her very nice home in rich Jewish suburbia and took an overdose.

Hedy's mom, my Aunt Fanny, seemingly had made a deadly decision regarding her estate that would have unforeseen consequences: She named Uncle Louis executor. From all accounts of those in the know, following Fanny's passing, he withheld monies from Hedy, claiming instead that he was preserving the inheritance for her two children. Not trained for anything in particular, Hedy had valiantly tried running a flower shop, but struggled.

Before her suicide, she apparently mailed a letter of reprisal. I was more confrontational. Standing outside my uncle's London flat many years later I mentioned matter-of-factly: "I hear, you wouldn't give Hedy her own money." Just as matter-of-factly, Louis responded: "I couldn't Gee; she was going to use the money to buy a house with that woman, that lover of hers. I couldn't stand for that."

Hedy was regarded by her mother as "highly-sexed." True, as kids, she always wanted us to go to her room and kiss and cuddle. Her mom also expressed concern about the number of Cokes she consumed. Hedy lined up king-size bottles of Coca-Cola in perfect order around all corners of her room; when one was empty the next container moved quickly up in line. She also was the proud owner of six little chicks that she kept in a cardboard box on the balcony and took out whenever I came by.

Most fun we enjoyed together was "general knowledge." Whenever we both stayed home with a cold or the flu, we phoned each other and played for hours. We drew up different categories on paper: animal, vegetable, mineral, cars, etc., and then went through the alphabet naming items under each. It took hours. If Auntie Fanny was out, she beseeched her next door neighbor Billie Cool—great name, huh—to pound on the door, demanding Hedy hang up.

Hedy adored her father, my Uncle Maish, the shy radiologist. And believed he equally worshipped his little girl. I'm not so sure. One visit as we all stood in the kitchen, Fanny told him Hedy had been cheeky to her and also their nanny, Anna. That Anna, with the long teeth, was without doubt, the surliest, sulkiest maid, white, black or colored in Africa. Suddenly Maish raised his hand and swatted Hedy as though she was a nuisance fly. She fell to the floor, wailing. My mother looked upset, but Fanny blew a curlicue of smoke as though nothing had transpired. Hedy ran away three times. And Uncle Maish apparently absorbed too much radiation on the job and died of leukemia.

Hedy was incredibly talented, and could play the drums and tap dance and won many medals at competitions. She was the soul of the party whenever the family got together. In talent, chutzpah and looks she surely preceded Madonna, what with that space between her front teeth.

Skittels married before me. She met a nice accountant named Jules, and soon had a daughter and then a son. Obviously, her family was not enough. The hurt won out. After my cousin Hedy's death, her religious daughter pondered whether her mother would ever have enjoyed being around grandkids. Mostly, she believed, Skittels feared getting old. So it was hardly surprising that she should take her life at age 39.

KADDISH

During the 1992 Los Angeles riots I long for my mother.

Staffers at the Los Angeles Times downtown where I work have been receiving calls from anxious mothers and fathers, brothers and sisters wanting to know how they're faring. As usual, no calls about my welfare.

Not even when it becomes known that in an attempt to keep order the mayor has imposed a curfew on a city torn apart in the wake of a globally-televised police brutality.

I leave the Times building in the early afternoon that first day to buy water, flashlights, batteries—emergency supplies normally reserved for earthquakes—at a Beverly Hills market. By 3 p.m. chaos reigns in the parking lot as silver Mercedes honk at green metallic Jaguars acing black BMW's into marked slots. Meanwhile, bagels and breads and deli salads disappear from shelves as though the dog days of war reign.

Sitting later on the patio of my Westside apartment, far from the madding strife, I realize that for once, everyone I know in the city remains home and reachable by phone. But still no calls from abroad.

This state of grace soon will lapse. On Saturday morning of Memorial Weekend I awaken to the sound of my phone machine answering in the adjacent den. I hear my cousin Belle urging me to call Johannesburg at once, followed by several messages from my brother. I know it's the end; I know my mother, with whom I have barely communicated in close to ten years, is dead.

Strangely, during the preceding weeks while driving on the Santa Monica Freeway to work, I heard a voice saying, simply, "Your mother's going to die." I took no notice. Then, a rarity: a letter arrived from my mother. She was following up on a rumor from an aunt who had recently visited me that I might be coming to Johannesburg.

"It would be so lovely to see you again," she wrote, adding that she had bought a pair of bright pink sheets for the single bed she'd surely rent should I come to stay.

For months I've been crying to a therapist at her penthouse rooms in Century City that I fear my mother, at 82, is getting really old and I really need to go back to South Africa and see her one more time.

No need to rush.
But how will I know when it's time to go?
You'll know.

My desperation in the first hours upon hearing the news is to say Kaddish. What else do you do with yourself when you know you can't make the funeral, half-way around the world? Iris Schneider, a photographer friend from the Times—we've worked together on many stories—arrives with a prayer book, and begins calling all the famous feminist rabbis she knows in the city. They're all away for the weekend. The one who does answer has hurt her back and my *mazel*, can't move, let alone come over to officiate. And there's no hope of assembling the required prayer quorum. So we just light a candle and open a bottle of Manischewitz wine left over from Passover a month earlier. Dressed in my finest velvets, wearing a white yarmulke, and with reading glasses so misty I barely decipher the print, I pray.

In ensuing days, I notice something strange. I'm truly living in the present, a rarity indeed. Work, friendships, politics, life as I generally know it, has nothing to do with me. Only her death feels immediate. I establish a new routine. Every morning I sit at my lovely white-tile table and light up a ciggy (I don't normally smoke), pour myself a cup or two of the remaining Manischewitz, and light the pink candles I normally reserve for the Sabbath. Then I pray or yell at God. Somehow the Kaddish and sweet red wine comfort me.

I commit to observing the ritualistic year of mourning. But Jews make it hard on a woman to honor the dead. Jewish law mandates that only a son may mourn out loud the life of a parent—only a son's prayers offer redemption. But I remain determined each evening to attend synagogue—any shul—and say Kaddish. First I try Beth Jacob, an Orthodox congregation in Beverly Hills. Seated behind a pale green trellis at the back of the room I remain hidden from the men chanting in a rapid-fire Hebrew I can barely follow. I'd do far better, advises the gray-haired, blue-suited assistant, to rather give $200 and have the synagogue, "Remember Madder."

"But will you say her name?" I'm desperate to hear someone honor Mary Beigel.

"No, but we will think of Madder as we pray, " he says. And if I write a check right there and then he'll notify me of the anniversary of her death.

Searching for any comfort zone I luck upon Temple Beth Am, a Conservative temple in the mid-Wilshire district of LA, where, at sundown, a group of kindly old men welcome me to their prayers and allow me my voice.

"Tonight we welcome Ms. Beigel who has lost her dearly-departed mother," Rabbi K. begins. Trouble is he articulates each word of every prayer in a sonorous voice at a sluggish tempo allowing for no deviation. Retired, he's found a calling leading the newly-bereaved along a nurturing path. Then there's 80-year-old Irving, a natty dresser in matching vest, suit and skull cap, who tries hard assuming a leadership role. He likes showing pictures of his wife of more than 30 years—"isn't she a beauty?"—as well as shots of himself as a lightweight boxer in shiny shorts of yesteryear.

In the sweetest tenor I've ever heard Irving calls out the page numbers in the prayer book. "On page such and such you'll find the 'Amidah'," he says. "And turn to page such and such for the 'Aleinu'." Then he calls upon the mourners to rise. My adrenaline starts its rush to recite the Kaddish.

Magnified and Sanctified
May His Great Name Be...

Reading the transliteration—I speak no Hebrew; in the South Africa of my upbringing only boys studied the language usually in preparation for their bar mitzvahs—I gradually become familiar with the phrases, accents and singsong intonation of the Kaddish. Miraculously, the prayer never speaks a word of death, but rather remains in praise of God.

Gradually, the Kaddish and I grow stronger. The prayer accepts my *fortissimos* and *pianissimos*; and tolerates my sometimes-impatient tempi and my exaggerated cadences and sighs and tears. After a mere six months, I thank Temple Beth Am by donating $100 towards a music scholarship fund. Finally, I'm ready to take my Kaddish on the road, ready to say the prayer with other congregants in Joh'burg. Mostly, I despair for some kind of closing ceremony, hoping to find peace at the "unveiling" of the tombstone at my mother's grave.

All the while, I continue editing film copy, readying all the movie reviews for the important Friday weekend section.

My editor grants a month's leave from the Times. Prior to my departure, I consult the bereavement experts at the Grief Recovery Institute at their West Hollywood offices. They suggest I have a private, mini-ceremony beforehand, and surround the burial site with artifacts recalling my mother's life.

It proves eerie to land at Jan Smuts Airport in Johannesburg (renamed O.R. Tambo International in 2006), and find no curious relatives and friends—so different to an earlier visit when I was scrutinized for changes in persona. "She's become so brash; a typical American," one socialite had concluded.

Talk about feeling alone. I wish Mommy were here; I'd prefer her wrinkled nose of disapproval at my hair and clothes to this aching void. A taxi drops me in the northern suburbs to register at the quasi-luxurious Sandton Sun Hotel. My high school friend, Phyllis, whom I have not seen in centuries, waits in the lobby.

"Hi Gret," she says in a sweet falsetto between puffs. I'm glad she's all blonde and slim and sexy. The next morning she picks me up at 9, and takes me to the cemetery for a makeshift ceremony, a ceremony of the absurd, an unforgiving Phyllis later attests. But then she's kind and understanding and sits with me on the gray slab of the poor dead and buried woman adjacent to my mother's still sandy plot. Discarding my green linen jacket under the hot November sun, I turn on the cassette recorder and play a song that my mother had adored and performed when pressured at countless family gatherings. Truth is, she had at her fingertips but three works: "Blue Danube," "Fascination," and "Velia" from Lehar's "The Merry Widow," which she'd play and/or sing over and over at home with a blank look on her face. In her memory, a soprano voice now warbles from the cassette player, "Vel-ia, oh Veee-lia..," as a group of startled gravediggers look up. In retaliation Phyllis shows up 40-minutes late and at the tail end of the Sunday morning memorial.

The rabbi, loathed in life by my mother, but nevertheless hired in death by my brother, eulogizes my mother as a woman who suffered. "Oh, how she suffered," he cries, "just like Sarah." I later ask a LA psychotherapist/author who specializes in Jewish mourning what this reference to Sarah's suffering could possibly mean.

"It doesn't mean shit."

At the graveside I ignore my brother's reaching hand. The day before he'd prescribed that only he, the son, publicly be permitted to pray. I lean heavily instead on Uncle Louis now in his 80s. As my left leg shakes uncontrollably, I wail inconsolably, on and on until he finally suggests, "I think it's enough Gee."

"Da daughter vas not at da funeral," the rabbi my mother hated explains to the more than 20 onlookers all shading disapproving eyes.

Suddenly, without pause or warning I hear the glorious declamation of the Kaddish. Standing as tall as I can muster, I recite each word, loud, proud and at my own speed and heard by all.

"Vot do you tink," the rabbi muses. "Da daughter says Kaddish for da Mother." Beaming, he turns to me: "Good for you, daughter."

Unbeknownst to all, the next morning I hire a taxi and return to the grave. I need one more goodbye, and throw myself on the stone, sort of a la Madonna when she visited her mother's plot in her film, "Truth or Dare."

"Oh Mommy, if you only knew how much I loved you," I cry. Even then, I feel her scorn rising up to meet the heat that morn. I also stop by my Dad's plot, although hardly in the mood for him just then. And I visit my cousin Skittels. She should never have departed without talking to me about it first. Never Skittels.

Joining the land of the living, I arrange to meet my nanny whom I have not talked to in decades. Kweekie had loved my mom—often though after a fight she'd disappear for months—until the very end. Even on her days off, Kweekie came into the city from Soweto and the two relaxed in the park nearby my mom's flat. Apparently they spent hours contemplating death, even fantasizing about one day sharing a grave. With segregation newly abolished, my mother treated Kweekie to meals and afternoon teas at restaurants in multicultural Yeoville where students soon flocked and where my mom resided for 40 years.

We agree to meet outside Bedford Pharmacy, the bustling corner establishment that Uncle Louis had owned years earlier. As the taxi drives up, I spy Kweekie, plump, aproned and anxious waiting for me. We go to the Black Steer, a steakhouse I'd frequented with my mother all those years before. But Kweekie has little hunger this day. She speaks nervously about prevailing hardships in Soweto and dangerous train rides. All the while she clutches a fading, crinkled plastic bag bearing the insignia Harrods.

I attempt to give her 200 Rands, the local currency.
"Not yet," she whispers. Then, as the meal ends: "Quick, give it to me now." I pass the notes along; she gromps the bills in a fist, before dropping the prize into the bag.

Kweekie comes again into the city to wave me a farewell. I've booked passage out on the posh Blue Train. At the dirty, bustling station armed guards patrol deserted platforms, before the train, all gleaming and blue pulls in from Pretoria.

Little blue mats suddenly materialize and a porter, dressed in blue, struggles to place my Samsonite into the single compartment replete with blue mat and blue sofa. With barely time for a quick hug and a goodbye comes the clarion call that thrills: "ALL aboard," and we depart the dangers of Joh'burg to glide gradually and through the desert, towards the greener pastures of the Cape.

I WANT MY MUSIC BACK

Months after my mother's death, I experience a strange longing to touch a keyboard. "Your trouble is, you need to create at the piano instead of writing about it," a colleague suggests.

I want a piano, but for whatever reason it has to be white. I rent an upright, telling myself I can stop if it proves painful. Pouring buckets of rain that Saturday when I visit Merrill's Music Shop in Santa Monica, I experiment at several pianos, attempting but the first five bars of a Mozart Rondo. Sixteen years at the bloody piano, and that's all I can remember.

An upright feels horribly restrictive to me, and soon I tire of the rented white Samick. I want a baby grand, fast, but still it must be creamy white. I think the obsession began after being exposed to the bejeweled white fantasy belonging to Liberace that I'd seen on display at a hotel lobby in Kalamazoo, Mich., where I'd reported on the Gilmore Festival.

Several musicians suggest I try different models at piano shops. I transport my few bars of the Mozart Rondo to Steinways and Baldwins, Bechsteins and Schimmels. Seated in front of each grand, I feel more expansive, feel the strength come down from my shoulders. With every breath there emerges a surge of power. I try out the fabulous Fazioli at a store in downtown Boston with my friend Logos, a Shanghai Conservatory-trained pianist who doubles as a successful businessman in LA.

I call him one morning hysterical over an ad in our paper. Appears the Hard Rock Café in Beverly Hills plans to raffle a Kawai baby grand, a white one. With the Times as co-sponsor, the event remains closed to me. Logos agrees to buy a ticket on my behalf; I'll pay applicable taxes should we win. From 6 p.m. we stand in a long line snaking around the restaurant and chat with a young woman in a tight white T-shirt ahead of us, passing time. Well, our ticket's pulled and nets us Hard Rock T-shirts as runners-up; Miss Tight Tits wins the piano. She doesn't even play; it's for her friend. We both cry into our salads, Logos the hardest. "This is the story of my life," he sniffs, "I'm always coming in second."

Time to head for the Hollywood Bowl for a press conference. Because the LA Philharmonic's very clever publicity director, my friend (the late) Norma Flynn always catered a good spread for the media, I arrive early and well before management offers its customary self-congratulatory remarks about the upcoming season.

Standing on the apron looking out at the deserted arena, I feel a shocking surge of familiarity. "Oh no you don't," I glare up at the sky. With no one looking, I take a bow, imagining my left hand at its customary position on the flattened music stand of a Steinway as I graciously lower my head.

Soon Van Cliburn will occupy that very stage making his first Bowl appearance in 18 years, playing the Rachmaninoff Third and Tchaikovsky First concerti on the same bill. I interview the nearly 60-year-old Cliburn at his luxury suite at the Four Seasons Hotel in Beverly Hills. How long ago it all seems when I sat on the patio in South Africa dreaming of coming to America and perhaps meeting this pianist, my idol.

Cliburn confides about his hopes for a triumphant comeback; I confide my despair about playing again. He instructs me to practice scales, scales, scales, and to my delight, demonstrates the desired touch on my back. Mostly, it gives me a good opening for my feature appearing in the Sunday Calendar section of the Times.

"I know in my bones you'll play again," Cliburn says, doing his best to sound sincere. Surely, few classical music stars ever mastered sincerity as did (the late) Harvey Lavan Cliburn, Jr.

Albeit hungering for something revelatory, almost every journalist resorts to rehashing the same worn-out tidbits, a few embellishments possibly aside, that Cliburn disseminated after winning the Tchaikovsky International and establishing his own quadrennial piano contest in Texas.

I journey to Ft. Worth to cover for the Times the Ninth Van Cliburn Competition. And breaking tradition from the many journalists lapping up freebies, pay my own way. With regularity, courtesy buses arrive to transport the media to yet another party at yet another rolling hills estate. Backstage, I watch writers and critics—between all of us we probably couldn't come up with a decent Mozart cadenza—tear contestants to shreds. And responding to gossip I hear on a bus, schedule an impromptu interview with the odds-on winner, Italian pianist Simone Pedroni, chatting with him under an umbrella on a folding green lawn.

Pedroni's words import a profound impact. Growing up in Italy, he says, music was the most natural thing in his household, almost like breathing, a part of the body. I later encounter this same natural-flowing phenomenon when interviewing for the New York Times pianist Byron Janis regarding his attempts to resurrect a career long-sidelined by crippling arthritis. Arriving early for a recording session, Janis toodled effortlessly—and magnificently—through a Chopin Scherzo as if to say good morning all and ran through a Mozart Concerto as if to add hi, my name is Byron. Playing the piano is mere extension of these artists; in my house, it ranked an elaborate and artificial set-up, designed to achieve a modicum of fame and glory.

For my first efforts at starting over, my friend Andrea brings over six books of simple pieces including the Anna Magdalena series by J.S. Bach. I relish the singing tone I produce by playing, for whatever reasons, with flat fingers, but quickly realize my technique's mostly kaput. As I increase speed, notes sound uneven. Although my hands are small, I used to work miracles around hurdles. Now octaves seem remote. The superduperfacility I had virtually been born with has vanished. What did I expect? I hadn't touched a note in 20 years. But still I'm disappointed.

Then I talk to a pianist severely injured in a fall while fixing a light bulb. He credits his rehabilitation to New York pedagogue Dorothy Taubman. I call a Times librarian for press clippings and plough through a wad of stories. I discover that Taubman trained several disciples around the country to work with injured musicians, including a well-known chamber musician in California. I find my way to Nina Scolnik, a glam pianist with long curly hair who serves on the faculty of the University of California at Irvine. She agrees to teach me privately at her Laguna Niguel home.

Remember some of the words to the spiritual song, "Dry Bones?"
The foot bone connected to the leg bone,
The leg bone connected to the knee bone,
The knee bone connected to the thigh bone,
The thigh bone connected to the back bone......

Well, with the Taubman approach, everything depends on a system of coordinated movement. Herewith a few notes

I jotted in my score of the first movement of Beethoven's First Concerto.

"The wrist mustn't be too high or too low but even, and each knuckle has to stand out just right and be coordinated with the elbow which mustn't be too high and the forearm must coordinate with the elbow..."

I feel compelled, even anxious, to write about my experiences with this approach. For the Times, I cover a two-week Taubman Institute where more than 200 keyboardists— performers, professors, would-be teachers, doctors, scientists, of all ages and from all backgrounds gathered in Amherst, Mass., for lessons and lectures and colorful master classes with the founder who made a lifelong study of the human anatomy. (Taubman died on April 3, 2013, in her mid-90s.)

The method works. Sort of. With Nina, attempting the Beethoven First, I achieve a certain evenness of speed that had been lacking. My octaves feel great, but still many passages remain beyond my humble reach. Mostly, Taubman's teachings prove complex and painstaking, sometimes even to the point of agony.

"If you knew you had eight years to study and then you'd be able to play again fabulously, wouldn't you say it's worth it?" Nina suggests more than once.

Meanwhile, The Times continues its efforts to accommodate all our injuries, eventually ordering adjustable chairs and tables and also footstools and wrist rests, and even building me an ergonomically-enhanced desk. Permitted a lighter work schedule, I write mainly advance features, thus avoiding the tightening under deadline pressure.

But nobody loves me for it. And not a day goes by when some fool doesn't comment on the pale blue wrist braces I must wear to type and/or edit. But I produce some fun pieces.

When the LA Philharmonic opens rehearsals to the public, I observe up-close an unshaven Esa-Pekka Salonen in black jeans, sport shirt and sneakers, conducting Grieg's "Peer Gynt." From the front row I watch his stomach suck in at the crescendo then explode at climax, in and out, in and out. I think I'm gonna die. For the fashion section, I convene with the nation's top female conductors about their dress codes, and we run some pleasing pictures of Gisele Ben-Dor, Catherine Comet, JoAnn Falletta and Iona Brown in tuxes and tails and loose-fitting gowns.

I also call Germany to chat with my favorite young violinist Christian Tetzlaff. All this before my genius editor—you know the one who admits he knows nothing about music but is great at sports—concocts a story about opera singers and what they do when they get the flu. Mezzo Frederica von Stade takes aspirins, Marilyn Horne has a humidifier going 24/7 in her New York pad and Simon Estes stocks up on vitamin C. Gee whiz. But do you know what it was like to have Pavarotti's manager threaten to hang up at such stupidity?

The Times, like many corporations in America in the mid-'90s, begins restructuring and reorganizing, downsizing and uploading and offering a series of buyouts. Turns out, I'm not eligible. Then along comes some new hotshot CEO fresh from a stint heading a cereal company.

Rumors quickly spread in editorial about a pending purge. One thing I've learned in my nearly 12 years on staff is that rumors at the LA Times almost always run true. Some mucky-muck upstairs just can't resist spilling the beans. Reporters, as is their wont, gather in clusters several times daily to speculate on any gloomy forecast. I'm scheduled to fly to Switzerland to do a freelance magazine piece on a music festival opening at Verbier, a ski resort in the Alps. After pressing the send button on the last piece I've written before my trip, a profile about Julia Cameron, author of the "Artist's Way," I just pray I'll get to depart the building before Doomsday.

The way things transpire, I'm scaling one mountain top in Switzerland when Black Friday hits. Or is it Bloody Friday when hundreds of jobs, and eventually thousands at Times Mirror facilities across the nation, are eliminated.

Given my limitations, it's hardly a surprise upon my return from Europe to find myself on the list. But I'm pissed off when a lawyer friend back East deems the move good for Times Mirror stock.

With a severance payment in the bank, I leave LA as speedily as humanly possible and head to Boston to dabble in a bit of musical esoterica. I'm on my way, or so I believe, to getting my music back.

A Boston Lament

I knew this was the wrong move.

For some time now piano teacher Nina, concerned about my wayward rhythmic impulses, has been touting a discipline she explored as a student called Dalcroze Eurhythmics. Espoused at many academies and conservatories, especially in Europe, Dalcroze teaches about rhythm, via movement and song and even tossing a ball or two this way and that. It all sounds like fun and she thought might work in my favor.

Again, after researching press clips, I learn that one Jacques Dalcroze founded a school in his name, now headquartered in Geneva. While on my visit to Switzerland, I take two trains and pop in to the academy. The director invites me to attend a dance demonstration.

My reaction's immediate: I hate it, even panic watching the choreographed, albeit strange rhythmic give and take between participants. Hurriedly I abandon the air-conditioned auditorium for the spanking clean pastry shop next door where I gorge on five miniature éclairs until I calm down. But do I register my body's revolt and go home? Nooooo. Instead I descend upon the premier Dalcroze exponent from the States strutting her stuff at the Geneva conference, and promptly decide to move to Boston to study with her.

My pianist friend Logos offers to take me to the airport. He arrives at my apartment hours before, carrying of all things, a huge white bedspread that his friend Kathy wanted me to have. What the hell do I need that for? I cringe as Logos stuffs the white monster into my already bulging bag.

My American Airlines flight lands at Boston's Logan at 7 p.m. I'm anxious to get an early taxi to my teacher's house where I'll stay for a few weeks. Waiting at baggage claim, I observe suitcase No. 1 tumble cheerily down the chute; black bag No. 2, with unwanted bedspread emerges busted, apparently patched together by airline personnel with miles of shining silver duct tape.

Host Lisa guffaws viewing the mess, and we both drag the monster into her garage where it rests, unopened, until I eventually find my own place. Was the busted bag a bad omen, I keep wondering? Should I have come?

There are opposing camps of opinion about Boston: Historians and scholars deem it the greatest, the closest to a European capital you'll find in the United States what with its sense of history and place and trains and stone buildings and cemeteries, all seeped in a glorious tradition.

I don't care about its zillion Early Music ensembles playing at a zillion churches throughout. I resent having to take sometimes two trains to get to Brookline in search of hot matzo ball soup, especially when with cold. And I find it irritating that few in the city or the state for that matter acknowledge, or even give a damn about the Academy Awards. At least in LA, comes Oscar-time there's always someone to talk to. And should someone attractive serve you at an eatery you know he/she's an actor-in-waiting. In Boston, the snooty help usually are Ph.D. candidates waiting to get through school.

However, to my surprise, I find great inspiration amidst the green pastures and environs of Harvard's Divinity School. One particular October Yom Kippur resonates. In the very late afternoon of this Day of Atonement I buy a cup of coffee and a muffin and break the fast alone sitting on a concrete wall, surrounded by flowers at the School quadrant. Here, dorms encircle the gardens where squirrels debate and nice, kind students studying God always smile. The big blue birdbath hosts feathered friends stopping by to sip in the hot summers, or to chat amidst the leaves of browns and golds and orange in God's own autumn.

Soon I frequent Harvard Hillel, a giant glass-domed structure offering Orthodox, Conservative and Reform synagogue services. In a generous departure, doors remain open to the community. At a Friday night Reform service, I meet Jerry, a fiftysomething and very bulky-looking theory of music teacher who has been on staff at the New England Conservatory of Music for decades. We become friends, often attending free concerts at the Longy School of Music in Cambridge, where I've registered for some classes.

Known for its community outreach, Longy's rated one of the top Dalcroze stations in the country. Mostly, I err in thinking I'll find a musical salvation there. Instead, the highest standard of learning awaits me across the street at Harvard, where the Extension division offers several music courses, including one in theory and composition. Throughout the freezing winter weeks, Prof. John Stewart encourages all sorts of musicians—good, bad, jazz, classical, pop, rock—to reach their true potential. He revels in the joy of all music, and I quickly respond. He shows us tricks as a way to recognize intervals, and I feel the rust in my psyche slowly starting to crank. For instance, the "Dooo-do, doooo-do" theme from the film "Jaws," represents a Minor Second. "Ma...ria" from "West Side Story" constitutes an Augmented fourth, and the theme from N---BC (television), a Major Sixth. Prof. Stewart reinforces my belief that creativity flourishes amidst play.

Observing two squirrels running around in Harvard Yard, I compose for class the "Squirrel Song," in 3/4 time, marked allegro and modulating to another key or two. For our final assignment, we must present an original piece based on our own writing or a famous poem or work of literature. I'm stymied, until the day I meet young South African friend Belinda for lunch. Tired of my complaints,

Belinda who is studying in the city insists: "But what is wrong with Boston?"

Trudging through snow now turned to dangerous sidewalk slush, I hear her words echoing over and over. Soon I have my theme. Rushing home, and in less than an hour I notate, "A Boston Lament," an accounting of my life in song and verse and filled with Fiddler on the Roof-type inflections.

The class decrees my saga a possible mini-Broadway musical; the good professor concludes I might do well amongst the New York avant-garde theater scene. He gives me an A.

HANG UPS

Boston four years later: I need to escape my brother. He's tracked me down. At least that's how he puts it. Actually he instructed his son to scour the local phone listings. Big deal. When I left the Times I hinted I'd go either to New England or New York. I'm home with the flu when my brother calls. "Jesus Christ where've you been. Lizzen my girl, I have to know where you are at all times." To this day if anybody says this phrase, I shudder. Not a good idea to use those words on me.

And although he calls but a few times a year to wish me happy birthday, a happy Passover or each fall, a good Rosh Hashanah and well over the Fast, each conversation takes its toll. I post yellow notes on my computer and all over the walls: "If he calls, say I'm busy, HANG UP." Yet I cannot accomplish that reality. No matter how hard I try, I still make pointless childish chatter. "Oh...... Boston is so cold." Then hate myself for days.

But I find my Truth where I always do—via journalism. I read a New York Times article wherein the stepdaughter of Sandinista leader Daniel Ortega claims to have been sexually molested from age 11 and during her father's presidency. In her 30s at the time of the interview, she describes still being harassed, this time verbally during Ortega's suggestive almost nightly phone calls. She depicts her struggles to disconnect from such abuse.

"It seems simple now, but it took me a long time to learn to hang up that phone," she tells reporter Mirta Ojito. "First, I would say I was busy or I would pretend someone was with me. Then, I just stood there, quietly. Eventually, I slowly dropped the receiver..."

Damn. What courage (that clip remains an inspiration, and part of my permanent files). If she could do it, so can I. Days before Dec. 29, when I know He'll call to say howzit and wish me a happy birthday and put the kids on the line, I depart for Australia and New Zealand, leaving no forwarding phone number or address.

I'm gone.

TRANSFORMATION

After leaving the Times, I get out of LA fast and embark on a quest to find nirvana, that perfect place to call home. Along the way, I get my story down.

One hot August noon lunching on a feta salad at a blue taverna on the Greek isle of Kos, I shed tears for my father. Nodding, the kindly owner plies me with several cups of strong Nescafé doused with rich crème. Oh, that coffee.

From cozy quarters at a bayside inn on Orcas, one of the magical San Juan Isles north of Seattle, I first jot about encounters with my brother. I also think of him while attempting to play soccer, with a duck and a little orange ball, on the banks of the River Avon in that very-British city of Christchurch, NZ. How my *bootie* had relished those rugby/soccer matches growing up.

Covering up one chilly April afternoon on the pink sands of a beach in Bermuda, I recall twilights spent relaxing with my mother on the Durban shorefront, combing her hair and listening to her hard-luck stories. I remember her while sipping coffee at the (then) Hard Rock Café in a shopping mall in Reykjavik, Iceland, and later when revisiting my school years with friend Julie—for whatever reason I call her Julie Face; she dubs me Greta Face—now living in Melbourne, Australia.

Following my mom's passing in 1992, I find a solace scribbling at the Victoria & Albert Waterfront in Cape Town, a touristy spot touting the usual seafood eateries and overpriced gift shops.

Whenever things appear too tragic, I distract myself with new climes and mountains, oceans and vistas on travels that these last few years have taken me from Africa to Australasia and throughout parts of Europe and across America.

At the suggestion of pianist Byron Janis and wife Maria, I spend some quiet time and learn a bit about Vespers and things at a Benedictine monastery in Connecticut (after two weeks I scream for the sight of a rabbi). There, I realize the courage to sever all contact with my brother and his brood.

Again, and this time acting on a recommendation of a religious music therapist based in London, I board two trains into Normandy to pray, in French, with monks and nuns at the gray Abbey Blanche. Emboldened, I return to America to ready my book.

Visiting Las Vegas I edit some essays from my hotel suite on the Strip. Whenever those old familiar feelings surface, I rush downstairs to the casino, finding a strange comfort amidst all the cacophonies. At a motel some 90 miles to the south in the dusty gambling town of Laughlin I complete the memoir's first draft. There, I rescue a powdery brown-and-white cat that hangs around the motel and becomes injured in a raccoon attack. I rush her to a neighboring town for treatment, and friends near Vegas agree to take her in. For just two weeks, mind you. It's been more than ten years…

My little Ketzela—they name her Miss Kitty, she also answers to Meeow Meeows—proves the inspiration for a whimsical and educational audio CD/e-book I later create and call, *"Mewsings: My Life as a Jewish Cat."* Here, a devout calico pontificates on what it takes to be a good Jew in modern times, especially during the High Holidays and including Hanukkah.

For a time, I also experiment with settling in New Zealand, a sometimes-magical land of mostly chilly temperatures and landscapes and mountains and fjords and glaciers. I start off in Auckland, and there interview for the New York Times Prime Minister Helen Clark, a third-term leader and champion of the arts (she goes on to a career at the United Nations). I also spend time in the town of Nelson in the South, and even take steps to obtain my legal residency. But I miss America.

Sojourning sometimes in semi-sweet Hawaii, I revel in the beauty of pink and purple blooming bougainvillea, and become positively sexual whenever balmy breezes blow. In record time, I'm part of a nice Jewish life in bustling Honolulu and for the first time ever join a synagogue, actually plunking down $$$ for membership dues. Saturdays, I attend morning Shabbat services at Sof Ma'arav, a conservative shul where participation rules and congregants, in true island style, sport sandals and flowery shirts and skirts, even printed yarmulkes and transport all in flowery bags. I also participate in High Holiday services, enduring the nightly dive-bombing of mosquitoes as we continue our prayers for peace.

Early on I become enamored of one learned *davener*—call him cantor Ken/color him complex. Mostly, I'm mesmerized by his lyrical voice, a Jewish Pavarotti if ever I heard one. In-between posturing with the synagogue's many powers-that-want-to-be my cantor applies for freelance gigs, sometimes securing singing engagements in faraway places during Rosh Hashanah and Yom Kippur.

He indicates he's considering a possible position that's opening up in Ashland, Oregon; you know, home of the famed Shakespeare Fest. Perhaps I too should consider a move. As is my wont, I jump at this mere suggestion and in weeks am ready to relocate. I register for music and writing courses at Southern Oregon University. Soon I become friends with Vishal, the kindly young proprietor of the Flagship Inn nearby. He rents me rooms whilst I study and write. The good cantor, however, decides to stay home. In Hawaii.

I'm here to caution: a) Humans cannot live on Shakespeare alone; b) Sometimes there's no point going back to school—past longing/reasoning no longer resonates.

B-O-R-E-D, I move my king bed and few bags north to Portland—that little-big-city or is it big-little-city?—touted for its bicycles, breweries and valiant vegan food carts. Oh, how impressive the programming of the Oregon Symphony. And what creative zeitgeist permeates this rainy environment where ideas pop up and works come easily to fruition.

But Hawaii rests forever gentle on my mind. Awed by beauty, buffeted by blustery trade winds and ever-nourished by the sea, sun—and of course, pineapple, papaya and coconut—I often reflect there on a little poem I wrote at age 7 and completed when I turned 32.

"The moon is up
The stars are bright,
The wind is fresh and free
I look up at the sky
And know that God loves me..."

Right??

THE END

CPSIA information can be obtained at www.ICGtesting.com
Printed in the USA
LVOW07s1926090816

499663LV00001B/62/P